Digital Startups in Transition Economies

Agnieszka Skala

Digital Startups in Transition Economies

Challenges for Management, Entrepreneurship and Education

palgrave
macmillan

Agnieszka Skala
Faculty of Management
Warsaw University of Technology
Warsaw, Poland

ISBN 978-3-030-01499-5 ISBN 978-3-030-01500-8 (eBook)
https://doi.org/10.1007/978-3-030-01500-8

Library of Congress Control Number: 2018958887

This Palgrave Pivot imprint is published by the registered company Springer Nature Switzerland AG
The registered company address is: Gewerbestrasse 11, 6330 Cham, Switzerland

Dedicated to Polish startupers

Contents

List of Figures

List of Tables

Introduction

The presented work responds to the growing demand for a scientific approach to the phenomenon of startups (alternative spelling: start-up), which are a manifestation of the digital revolution and an economy based on innovation in the broadly understood use of information and communication technologies (ICT). The work discusses the economic phenomenon consisting in the emergence of this new form of organisation, presents the changes that accompany it, and indicates possible directions for further research in this area.

Taking up this subject was **motivated** by discovering the existence of a knowledge gap, manifested in an ambiguous understanding of the concept of "a startup" in the literature of the subject. That's why the results of research on startups are often incomparable, and the knowledge about startups is incomplete and fragmentary. At the same time, the hopes associated with the development of startups, understood as organisations initiating and commercialising innovations, are significant. The new, digitally advanced economy based on innovation is supposed to stimulate the sluggish and weakened by the financial crisis economies of developed countries, and startups are to be the agent of this positive change.

The definition dispute on what a "startup" is (and what it is not) is also ongoing in the business and investor community, as well as among the business environment institutions. Therefore, resolving this issue is not only scientifically important, but also significant from the point of view of business practice, because the scope and form of support provided to startups by various organisations, including public institutions, depend on the adopted interpretation of the "startup" notion.

At the same time, it is possible to see new directions of development in business management, created in the startup community and being perfected there, and now penetrating other industries and organisations seeking new methods for implementing innovation. Large companies, international corporations, and some public institutions implement innovation and development strategies, which consist in cooperation with startups—from free and non-committal relationships to very close cooperation and takeovers. The following examples from Poland can be cited here:

- stimulating the creation of startups in the area of specific solutions—for example, the financial industry initiative from BNP Paribas: "International Hackathon", which aims to create new solutions in the field of so-called FinTech,[1] that is, technologies that respond to new needs in the broadly understood financial industry; collaboration between PGNiG and the MIT Enterprise Forum startup accelerator promoting the development of startups related to the energy industry, or without specifying industries (including the creation of open spaces for all startup events: FabLab Polska by Orange, Campus Warsaw by Google, or the initiative of the Warsaw City Hall—Warsaw Technology Space);
- close cooperation with startups—for example, the insurance and financial group Aviva and the startup Airly work together on monitoring air quality; PKP S.A., a leading railway operator, and the startup Migam.pl, can provide together better service to deaf customers;
- takeovers of existing startups—for example, the purchase of the ZenCard startup by the PKO Bank Polski Capital Group, purchase of the Filmaster startup by the leader of the digital TV market Samba TV;
- investing in startups, also through own investment funds—for example, Hub:raum Kraków (T-Mobile), TVN Ventures, Witelo (PZU SA), Enea Innovation;
- launching internal startup projects in large corporations.

Finally, a startup as a new form of organisation and specific methods of managing startups affect educational institutions that educate "about

[1] Similar solutions appear in other specialisations, for example, "MarTech" solutions for the marketing industry, "InsurTech" for insurance, "EduTech" for educational, "MedTech" for medical.

startups" and "for startups" at the tertiary, secondary, and even primary levels. Effective education in this area requires an understanding of the key role of innovative entrepreneurship, which is important for economic development and the progress of civilisation. The new trend in entrepreneurship education is not to educate about how to set up your own business and to earn a living from it, but focuses on developing entrepreneurship attitudes oriented towards ambitious, dynamic, and global ventures.

The three areas of knowledge and competences mentioned earlier—startups, management, and education—reflect the scope and the layout of the presented work (Fig. 1). The listed subject areas affect each other, and the direction of development of each one affects the other two; therefore, the relations between them have a form of feedback.

The monograph consists of three chapters whose thematic scope and research objectives are presented in Table 1. The main **scientific goal** of the work is to introduce order into knowledge about startups.

Methodological triangulation was used in the project due to the complex, multifaceted nature of the subject. The study largely consisted of desk research, but a direct and open participating observation in the startup community was also an important source of knowledge and inspiration. It is worth noting that the research project was long enough to offset the effect of uncritical enthusiasm for the observed phenomena. The examples of startups cited in the work are based on author's own case studies used in her teaching practice. A large part of the analysis is also based on the primary quantitative and qualitative study "Polish Startups", co-created and coordinated (in cooperation with the Startup Poland Foundation) since 2015 by the author.

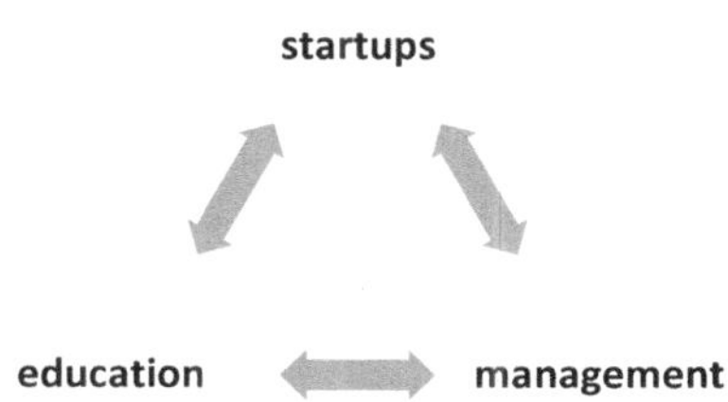

Fig. 1 The key issues triad in the startup entrepreneurship system. (Source: Own material)

Table 1 Scientific goal, questions, and research goals against the background of the structure of the work

Part of the work	*Thematic scope*	*Scientific objective*	*Research questions*	*Research goals*
Chapter 1	Startups—theoretical approach	Organising knowledge about startups	What is a startup?	Developing a universal definition of a startup
Chapter 2	Startups—an exploration approach		Startups as a subject of research in management and entrepreneurship sciences What are the characteristics of startups? Which features are most important in the characteristics of startups?	Critical analysis of the results of primary startup research in Poland Critical analysis of startups based on desk research
Chapter 3	Managing a startup in an innovation ecosystem and educating for startup entrepreneurship		What is the impact of startups on management? What is the specific nature of startup management? What is the impact of startups on management education? How to educate for startup entrepreneurship?	Conceptualisation and operationalisation of startup management methodology Assessment of the importance of startup management against the background of management science Developing guidelines for educators in startup entrepreneurship

Source: Own material

The author thanks everyone who contributed to the creation and improvements in this book. Special thanks are due to Professors Jerzy Cieślik and Janusz Zawiła-Niedźwiecki, as well as to my business partner Marek Kapturkiewicz. I would like to thank the "Startup Poland" Foundation for their continuous collaboration with the "Polish Startups" research project. Thanks are also due to my co-workers and friends who create startups or help them grow; thank you for dozens of interviews and conversations about startups and with startups, thanks to which I got to know this inspiring community.

CHAPTER 1

The Startup as a Result of Innovative Entrepreneurship

Abstract This chapter presents the characteristics of startups as a manifestation of innovative entrepreneurship in the era of digital revolution. The chapter concludes with a developed universal definition of a startup. First, the new market reality is presented, shaped as a result of the digital, social, and economic revolution, which resulted in the emergence of new, specific forms of organisation—startups. Next, the existing definitions of a startup are discussed and a model of startup development process is developed. These analyses are illustrated with examples of Polish and foreign startups. Finally, the concept of the so-called spiral definition of a startup is proposed.

Keywords Definition of a startup • Innovative entrepreneurship • Digital revolution • Disruption • Literature review

The purpose of this chapter is to carry out a critical review of different definitions of a startup found in the literature, and then to propose my own definition, taking into account a theoretical model of a startup development process considered as a manifestation of innovative entrepreneurship. This task also requires organising the most important concepts related to startups in the context of theories of management and entrepreneurship.

A. Skala, *Digital Startups in Transition Economies*,
https://doi.org/10.1007/978-3-030-01500-8_1

Although a growing number of scholars have been trying to capture and describe the unique specific characteristics of the startup phenomenon in recent years, there is still no general agreement as to what a startup is—both among scientists and business support institutions and among entrepreneurs themselves (Breschi et al. 2018). Originally, this concept referred to all new economic entities entering the market. Such a definition did not raise any controversy until the term began to be strongly associated with a specific category of enterprises connected to the dynamically developing information and communication technologies (ICT) sector, in particular the Internet, as a medium of universal, immediate, and virtually unlimited communication. These developments raised hopes in the context of increasing innovation and accelerating economic growth, especially in developed countries. A lack of precision in formulating the criteria for distinguishing these types of projects from other micro- and small enterprises may, for example, negatively affect the effectiveness of measures supporting the development of such projects implemented by various institutions (including public bodies) in many countries.

Regardless of the results of a detailed analysis, the concept of a startup is undoubtedly associated with running a business in its initial phases and with implementing innovations. Three groups of enterprises that can be initially classified as startups are of note. The first one includes projects from the so-called creative industries, that is, associated with creative design, crafts, and fine art. The second is entrepreneurship in science, that is, technology transfer and the commercialisation of inventions. Finally, the third group includes projects belonging to the so-called digital industry, where information processing technologies are one of the key elements in the business model. On the basis of these categories, this work will focus on the examination of the last of these three groups, because each operates according to different principles and they should not be considered together. The mechanisms of their functioning significantly differ for each of the startup categories and considering them together is not likely to result in a clear research process or a good analysis of the research results (Skala 2016).

Discussions and disagreements about innovative entrepreneurs and their role in economic development have been ongoing for nearly a century, inspired by the father of modern entrepreneurship—Joseph Schumpeter. On the other hand, startups are associated with a fundamental breakthrough in the economic, social, and even civilisational dimension, related to the spread of ICT (especially the Internet). The so-called new digital economy creates qualitatively new conditions for the functioning of startups. These issues will be presented and discussed first.

1.1 Entrepreneurship and Innovation

Joseph Schumpeter (1942) introduced the concept linking entrepreneurship with innovation to economic sciences. He defined "creative destruction" as a simultaneous combination of "creativity", "novelty", "innovation", and "development", and he defined entrepreneurs as—above all—innovators. Entrepreneurs, according to Schumpeter, are the agents of creative destruction, allowing the economy to experience changes that make progress possible and lead to the development of civilisation. He pointed out the power of innovation, which can destroy even the most durable corporations, and argued that the threat from radical (breakthrough) better solutions and new market entrants keeps the main players (currently the term "incumbents" is used) disciplined and willing to incur the costs of research and development investments, whose implementation leads to economic and civilisational progress, ultimately raising the standard of living of the lowest social classes (in the long run). According to Schumpeter, openness to innovation constitutes and distinguishes an "entrepreneur" from an "employee", while creative destruction consists in the emergence of new generations of innovators appearing as successive "waves" of innovation, which, although commercially obliterating the previous "generations", also generate added value in the form of an increasing (in absolute terms) quality of goods and services. It can therefore be said that the context of innovation is critically important for further consideration of startups as a new form of entrepreneurship.

Innovators and Imitators

Since Schumpeter, innovative entrepreneurial initiatives have been researched in conjunction with the entrepreneur as an individual, considered to be the catalyst and in possession of traits and skills that enabled innovation to be transformed into market value by creating new products and services (Shane 2003; Ács et al. 2009). Innovative entrepreneurs can be recognised by their unique ability and willingness to find and exploit new market opportunities (Wennekers and Thurik 1999). Certain individual characteristics of the entrepreneurs, their appropriate education, and access to specific resources (e.g. knowledge, tools, interpersonal networks) increase the likelihood of success (Shane 2000; Koellinger 2008). This direction of thinking was shared by Peter Drucker, recognised as a major authority in the field of management. He believed (1992) that only entrepreneurs who created new markets or implemented new solutions represented "real" entrepreneurship, regardless of the level of risk, the amount of money invested, or the number of jobs created. In contrast to this view, William Baumol (2010) valued the successes of imitators, that is, those who did not implement original solutions, but, thanks to minor improvements, often achieved better business outcomes than pioneers and innovators in the long run. This dispute remains one of the fundamental and unresolved questions in the area of entrepreneurship research and is related to the differences between small business and ambitious and dynamic (larger) business, as well as between innovators and imitators. Jerzy Cieślik (2017) extensively comments on this dichotomy, pointing out that it is reflected not only in academic research (different research methods and tools), but also in the sphere of economic policy (different objectives and instruments), while the issue of innovative business solutions is related to the level of entrepreneurial ambitions and the founders' breadth of vision. Cieślik points out that talking about innovative and ambitious entrepreneurs, as opposed to non-innovative and not ambitious ones, is a simplification and proposes a realistic model, more suited to Baumol's moderate views and thus recognising imitations and moderate entrepreneurial ambitions as important from the point of view of the development of entrepreneurship and the economy (Cieślik 2014a, p. 33). A similar position is represented by Block et al. (2017), who, aside from inventors and scientists, see sources of innovative entrepreneurship in the group of "demanding users" or proactive employees who create and implement relatively modest innovations.

This thread returns in the discussion about startups, because the majority of these do not create radically new solutions, but "improve" or copy existing ones, often achieving significant market success (e.g. Audioteka–Audible, Evenea–Eventbrite, Allegro–eBay)

Innovative Entrepreneurship and Economic Development

William Baumol formulated the concepts of productive, non-productive, and destructive entrepreneurship, which he defined in the context of the institutional environment in which organisations operate (1990). He claimed that entrepreneurship was an immanent human trait which—

depending on the "climate" in which it functioned—was creatively used or wasted. It is worth mentioning that until the beginning of the twentieth century, entrepreneurship was not associated with progress and socio-economic prosperity, and the first theories of entrepreneurship proposed by Richard Cantillon (1755) or Jean-Baptiste Say (1841) refer to it as a form of independent activity and the ability to notice and to take advantage of the market opportunity for exclusively particular benefit. As a result, as already mentioned, entrepreneurship was considered mainly in the context of characteristics and activities of the entrepreneur as an individual. Baumol divided the benefits of entrepreneurial behaviours into those that occur on a micro scale (at the level of a single enterprise) and those that affect the economy in the macro dimension (at the level of the national or global economy), whereby the enterprise's profit may or may not bring benefits for the economy.

The results of research by David Birch (1979 and 1987), which showed that small companies (not corporations) create the majority of new jobs in the United States, were a breakthrough in discussion about the role of entrepreneurship in the economy.[1] This provided the impulse for research on the impact of smaller-scale entrepreneurship on broadly understood economic development and prosperity. The conclusions, after nearly three decades of research, are still not completely unambiguous (Block et al. 2017), and reflect the division of entrepreneurship into "real" (innovative) and small business (and especially self-employment). While a small number of enterprises play the "breakthrough" role in the economy, the majority of people involved in creating new enterprises run subsistence businesses (Ng and Stuart 2016; Schoar 2010). Some research has demonstrated, for example, that new companies contribute strongly to job creation in Organisation for Economic Co-operation and Development (OECD) countries (Calvino et al. 2016; Criscuolo et al. 2014). Other studies have shown that a small number of successful breakthrough innovations, launched both by the incumbent companies and by fast-growing startups, are responsible for disproportionately higher increases in new jobs and productivity (Andrews et al. 2014). An OECD (2017) project DynEmp has shown that a very small percentage of startups develop really

[1] These conclusions were also undermined later—jobs are created mainly by young companies, not small ones (Haltiwanger et al. 2013), and the quality of these jobs remains problematic (Coad et al. 2013).

fast; for example, on average only 3% of newly created micro-enterprises employ more than ten employees after five years of operation. This is in line with earlier findings by Wong et al. (2005) based on the Global Entrepreneurship Monitor (GEM).

Thus, the impact of entrepreneurship on economic growth is usually indirect (Carree and Thurik 2008), and examining this relationship poses methodological difficulties. In a situation where the correlation between the level of gross domestic product (GDP) per capita and the level of self-employment is negative (Henrekson and Sanandaji 2014), while the vast majority of entrepreneurs do not hire staff at all and report minimal income (Shane 2008), real benefits for the economy are generated by a few innovative, fast-growing enterprises whose share in the total number of enterprises is estimated at a few (2–6%) per cent (OECD 2015). What's more, in the United States and in several other developed countries, a clear downward trend can be observed in the founding of new companies, and the overall dynamics of business growth (Blanchenay et al. 2017; Decker et al. 2016). At the same time, entrepreneurship financed by venture capital (VC) funds is growing, and the total amount of VC funds provided to startups in OECD countries in 2015 was 50% higher than in 2007. In the United States, a similar upward trend has been observed since 2014, as well as a growing number of so-called unicorns, that is, startups valued at at least US $1 billion (Guzman and Stern 2016).

In this context, and as a result of a negative evaluation of the effectiveness of many public programmes that aimed to stimulate economic development by supporting entrepreneurship (Rannikko and Autio 2016; Kösters 2010), the policy priorities of the countries promoting entrepreneurship are being reformulated. This can also be seen in Poland (Stępniak-Kucharska 2015). It is no longer about promoting entrepreneurship as such, but about precisely constructed instruments designed to support very specific projects, valuable from the point of view of the national economic policy. The most interesting case studies even demonstrate that real effects appear completely outside the mainstream of the so-called entrepreneurship policy, in areas such as education or social and health insurance (Fairlie et al. 2011).

Innovation and the Size of the Enterprise

Another creative dispute in the approach to innovative entrepreneurship also dates back to Schumpeter (1942), who claimed that larger companies are more predestined to implement innovations than smaller businesses (Scherer 1984). Evidence against Schumpeter's claim (presented further on) began a series of studies focusing on factors other than the characteristics of entrepreneurs themselves, which have a significant impact on the company's inclination towards innovative implementations, for example, company size (especially measured by the size of its workforce), sources of financing, access to specific resources, business environment, and others. Research on this subject was undertaken in the 1990s, focusing on the efficiency of expenditure on research and development in large and small companies (Ács and Audretsch 1990; Cohen 1995) or on bureaucratic barriers on the paths to innovative implementations in corporations (Utterback 1995; Christensen and Bower 1996), as well as verifying a hypothesis that big companies are attached to retaining their market status quo at the expense of entrepreneurial alertness (Christensen 1997). Conclusions from these studies pointed to an advantage on the side of smaller companies, where innovation was fostered by a greater operational flexibility, flat organisational structures, and an ability to more easily notice market niches often unattractive for large market players (Ács and Audretsch 1988, 1990). On the other hand, other authors emphasised that large organisations accumulate more knowledge that helps them to create innovation—although more often than not, incremental and non-revolutionary rather than radical (Henderson 1993). Josh Lerner (2004) examined innovation in companies providing financial services and unequivocally determined that smaller companies were more likely to introduce innovative solutions. Similar conclusions were obtained with regard to companies with academic connections and businesses operating in clusters, allowing them to take advantage of additional synergies (Elfring and Hulsink 2003; Baptista and Swann 1998; Eisenhardt and Schoonhoven 1996). It is also worth citing the results obtained by Burgelman and Sayles (1988), who draw attention to the diversity of processes that determine the successful implementation of innovations (combining technical, market, business, and production knowledge) and that the operationalisation of such diverse competences is easier in a smaller team.

One can also look at the "sluggishness" of incumbent companies from another perspective and see it as a market opportunity for new entrants. Significant clusters of large companies will generate demand for innovative enterprises in order to cooperate with them (Gans and Stern 2003) or for takeovers (Henkel et al. 2015; Dushnitsky and Lenox 2005). This kind of cooperation takes many forms, from the so-called hackatons[2] or competitions on a subject given by the corporations, to incubation,[3] excubation,[4] acceleration,[5] co-financing, to a takeover (Prats et al. 2017, p. 21).

The thesis that smaller business forms are better at commercialising completely new knowledge, especially in the early period, when it is still ambiguous, in a sense "fluid" (Audretsch and Keilbach 2004), was confirmed. This type of situation can now be observed in relation to pioneering attempts to commercialise solutions in the field of blockchain systems using cryptocurrencies (e.g. Bitcoin, Ethereum), which occur in the startup environment (examples of projects include Kraken, BitMarket, Coinroom), and not in the (traditional) financial services environment (banks and insurance companies so far have been using startup cryptocurrency services more often than creating them themselves).

1.2 Innovative Entrepreneurship in the Digital Revolution Era

Joseph Schumpeter could not have predicted that breakthrough ICT solutions implemented on a global scale would create an unprecedented advantage for smaller and younger companies, and even create a business space in which a startup can realistically threaten a powerful and prosperous industry (e.g. Airbnb in the hotel industry and Uber in the taxi market). The expansion of the computer industry, the sector of services related to software development, and, finally, the new space for information sharing via the Internet have brought significant changes not only in economic

[2] Hackaton is a multi-hour (e.g. two to three days without a break) event during which developers design IT solutions for a given problem or for a given industry (e.g. educational websites, applications for government agencies); a type of competition.

[3] Incubation is a free advisory and training service for enterprises at an early stage of development, often associated with the physical placing of the company in the so-called incubator, that is, in the place indicated by the organiser of the incubation programmes; for example, Academic Business Incubators and their co-working network: Business Link.

[4] Excubation describes incubation programmes, usually run by corporations, that do not contain an element of placing a startup in an incubator.

[5] Acceleration describes very intensive, 8–12 week-long educational programmes for startups that are to help them to quickly verify a business model; often a startup "pays" for the acceleration programme with its shares (about 5% of shares). Accelerators are in this case funds that invest at a very early stage of development; the most famous and the most prestigious accelerator in the world is YCombinator.

terms but also in terms of civilisation as a whole. ICT solutions have been recognised as so-called general purpose technologies (*GPT*), that is, technologies that radically and globally accelerate socio-economic development (cf. Hofmokl 2009). Universal and groundbreaking changes in almost every sphere of human activity caused by ICT developments have been described as a "digital revolution". This has also influenced entrepreneurship. Special forms of innovative enterprises—the startups—have become the agent of revolutionary changes, both implementing and commercialising new technical and technological solutions in the field of information processing.

"Software is eating the world", wrote Marc Andreessen[6] in his famous *Wall Street Journal* article (2011). He meant digitisation, that is, the increasingly common use of information processing technologies by people, which results in a thorough transformation of many (and ultimately all) areas of human activity. The main driving forces behind these changes are, above all, automation and robotisation, information gathering and processing technologies, as well as completely new communication channels. Automation comes the closest to the idea expressed by Adreessen, because it is the algorithms that are to replace humans in activities that can be "translated" into the language of mathematics. This is how, in simplified terms, software is created that replaces the work of the human brain, whereas robotisation mainly aims at replacing the work of human muscles by machines (although the boundaries between these concepts, especially in their interpretation, are quite blurred). In this context, it is worth mentioning cyborgisation which, thanks to a new generation of interfaces, that is, methods of communication between man and machine, will in the near future support human functioning. This is already happening due to the so-called bots, computer programmes that have already replaced human beings in certain tasks (e.g. a chatbot "pretends" to be a human during a sales-support conversation with a customer of an online store or a call centre) or through electronic subsystems implemented in the human body (Ciechanowski et al. 2018). Unlimited possibilities for collecting and

[6] Marc Andreessen (born 1971) is an American entrepreneur and investor, as well as a programmer. He is a co-creator and a managing partner of one of the most prestigious venture capital funds Andreessen-Horowitz, and is or was an investor and member of supervisory boards of leading e-business companies, such as Facebook, eBay, Skype, Zynga, Twitter, LinkedIn, and many others. He is considered to be a visionary in the field of the directions of development of the digital economy.

complex processing of huge data sets (*Big Data*, *data mining*) provide a completely new opening for the prediction and management of processes and their broadly understood modelling, decision-making support, and, in general, for achieving a comprehensive understanding of a complex reality. Digital communication used in business for customer communications provides previously unattainable insights into customers' needs and behaviours and, in combination with the previously mentioned trends, affects, for example, the development of the so-called mass customisation, that is, the production of short runs or even individual "bespoke" products tailored to the preferences of narrow segments of customers, which replaces the mass production of standardised goods and services "for everyone".

Completely new opportunities are opening up for entrepreneurs in the digital age, but numerous threats also emerge. Andreessen, quoted above, is a strong supporter of the claim that the advantages of digitisation outweigh potential losses. In the above-mentioned text, he dismisses the fear of another "Internet bubble" (after the 2000 one) and argues that the situation is just the opposite, because a new economy has developed around the Internet, providing highly profitable and fast-growing business models. It is based on knowledge and progress in the area of high technology—mainly in relation to information processing and communication technologies—which affects the entire economic system, increasing its efficiency. Andreessen thus claims that we are experiencing, in the language of W. Baumol, a constructive form of entrepreneurship. New branches of the economy are emerging which result in transformations, ultimately affecting all other sectors—that's why we are talking about the digital "revolution", not about a "change" or an "innovation wave". These changes are holistic in nature and are taking place on a global scale, and the principles of functioning of the whole economy and its individual elements are evolving. This also applies to the rules of competition, because the ability to collect, store, process, and, most importantly, use information determines market success (Borowiecki and Dziura 2016), which is what digital technologies do. In this context, it is worth discussing the concept of the so-called fifth wave of competition (Noga 2009)[7]

[7] Noga describes the successive waves of competition as follows: the first wave (Harvard school) was competition that relied on multiple market players and fighting monopoly; the second (Chicago school) focused on minimising (though not eliminating) state intervention

which is the result of the co-occurrence of several phenomena: globalisation, deregulation, technical revolution, and the "renaissance of consumer sovereignty". The fifth wave of competition is characterised by uncertainty and hyper-competition, and the key resources of enterprises are knowledge, talent, and capital. Small players, as has already been mentioned, can force even the largest, market-dominant corporations to react, and companies increase their profitability mainly thanks to their skilful use of intellectual capital.

Andrzej Wojtyna (2001) wrote in his widely cited text about the difficulties that await those who attempt to explain the phenomena characterising the new economy using the traditional economics toolkit (although he did not claim that it was impossible). He drew attention to the fundamental difference in the paradigm of the new economy, where not the scarcity of goods, but, on the contrary, the universality of their use and the number of users (consumers) define their value. He also accurately predicted the result in the form of markets where the *winner-takes-all* strategy applies. Jana Pieriegud (2016, p. 11) adds that "digitisation as a continuous process of convergence of the real and virtual worlds becomes the main engine of innovation and change in most sectors of the economy". These changes are often breakthrough in character (in other words, subversive, disruptive), meaning they completely change the market status quo on the demand as well as on the supply side. That's why the digital revolution is being defined as the "fourth industrial revolution" (otherwise Industry 4.0), consisting of three main phenomena. The first is universal digitisation, especially in the field of communication between people, people with machines, and machines with each other (so-called M2M, *machine to machine*). The second is disruptive innovation, which

in the economy. The discussion between the supporters of both classic schools continues to this day. Since the late 1960s and for the following two decades of the twentieth century, powerful geopolitical, social, and economic changes (e.g. oil crises) disturbed the established market status quo. The third wave of competition, focusing on the choice of the optimal operating strategy, emerged. The strength of competition was no longer decided by the state or the number of entities on the market—but by the ability to compete as a derivative of the adopted strategy. The fourth wave arose with the intensification of deregulation and privatisation of many sectors of the economy, which took place in the 1980s. The fourth wave competition allowed the optimal (rather than maximum) number of the best enterprises to operate on the market. The fifth wave comes with the breakdown of optimal market structures and their virtualisation.

rapidly increases the effectiveness of various (difficult to predict) social or economic subsystems. The third phenomenon is automation leading to the autonomy of devices thanks to control based on artificial intelligence (AI) (Paprocki 2016; Przegalińska 2016). A McKinsey report (Dörner and Edelman 2015) describes how managers understand digitisation: directly as an implementation of digital technologies, as a new opportunity to reach customers, and, in the broadest sense, as a completely new way of doing business. The last of these views lines up with the thesis behind this publication, indicating that a startup is a new form of organisation and at the same time an emanation of a digitising economy and a new system of social relations.

Placing startups on the map of the economy undergoing the digital revolution is also not easy, because digitisation affects the characteristics of technological entrepreneurship in general (Nambisan 2016). Ferran Giones and Alexander Brem (2017) propose a division into technology entrepreneurship, entrepreneurship in the field of digital technologies, and digital entrepreneurship (Table 1.1).

Each of the presented forms of entrepreneurship has its specificity and its own developmental dynamic, creating various trajectories of enterprise development: while under "pure technological entrepreneurship" (Brem and Voigt 2009) the entrepreneur was looking for applications and creating a demand for a completely new technology (Giones and Miralles 2015), digital technologies require a different approach, strongly

Table 1.1 Forms of technological entrepreneurship in the digital revolution era

Form	*Description*	*Examples*
Technological entrepreneurship	New products based on scientific breakthroughs	Graphene, blue laser, cancer vaccine, perovskites
Entrepreneurship in the field of digital technologies	New products based on ICT, Internet of Things, electronics, robotics	Smartphones, beacons, wearables, sensors
Digital entrepreneurship	Internet-based services and the concept of the so-called cloud, making a great use *of Big Data* and AI	Airbnb, Snapchat, Dropbox

Source: Own material based on Giones and Brem (2017)

demand-oriented (Priem et al. 2011). New digital entrepreneurs do not focus on technology, which is treated as a tool, an infrastructure, a unique resource—but not as a product. Services or material products are developed using this technology as a basis. The division into hardware and software gives way to hybrid solutions that integrate science, business, and technology.

The most important socio-economic trends presented so far illustrate the phenomena against which startups—new forms of innovative entrepreneurship—appeared. Using the typology of the most common forms of contemporary entrepreneurship proposed by Jerzy Cieślik (2014a, pp. 65–84), the area in which startups emerge (Fig. 1.1) can be mapped. Startups are thus innovative, ambitious, expansive, fast-growing, and focused on global markets. They feature a technological component associated with ICT solutions. They also occur in the corporate (*corporate*

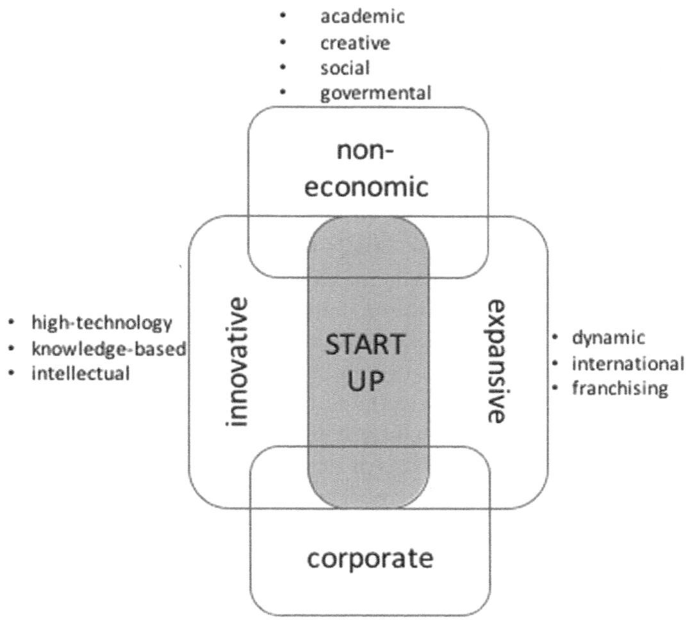

Fig. 1.1 Startups in the framework of contemporary forms of entrepreneurship. (Source: Own material based on Cieślik 2014a)

venturing) and non-economic spheres, for example, in the form of social entrepreneurship or in the public sector.

The next part of the chapter aims to organise the current knowledge on what startups are and what their distinctive characteristics consists of, as well as undertake the author's own interpretation of the phenomenon.

1.3 Startups: Literature Research

In the original sense, the word "startup" meant any form of business in its early stage of development (Breschi et al. 2018; Csaszar et al. 2006). Gradually, however, the connotation of this concept narrowed towards ambitious, dynamic, and technological undertakings, with the beginnings of this change dating back to the 1970s. According to the *Oxford English Dictionary* the first use of the word "startup" in the new meaning occurred in 1976 in the biweekly *Forbes*, where "the business of investing in the startups in the electronic data processing field" was mentioned.[8] A year later *Businessweek* dated 5 November 1977 mentioned "incubators for startups, operating in fast-moving industries related to high technology".

To understand and correctly carry out a search for the definition of a startup, it is worth highlighting the motivation behind the desire to undertake such a search. In 2015, the team preparing the first survey of startups in Poland (discussed in more detail in Chap. 2) faced the challenge of building a database of companies qualifying as startups. Such databases exist abroad (e.g. Crunchbase, used by numerous researchers: Breschi et al. 2018; Alexy et al. 2012; Bertoni and Tykvová 2015; Block et al. 2015). It became necessary to define criteria that would allow for identifying entities operating on the market as startups. Exploring the subject led to the identification of significant discrepancies in how the term "startup" was defined in literature and the resulting lack of explicitly formulated criteria for selecting a sample of startups. It is thus worthwhile to formulate such a definition, which will provide criteria for determining whether a given entity is a startup or not.

The most important and the most popular definitions are discussed in more detail later in this chapter. It should be noted here that in the case of startups, academic research significantly overlaps with the output of

[8] In the original: "the business of investing in the startups in the electronic data processing field"; Forbes, 15/08/1976, pp. 6/2.

experienced startup creators—available in a variety of forms and communicated using various, sometimes not obvious, channels of communication (e.g. personal communication or company blogs). What's more, selected representatives of the startup ecosystem—entrepreneurs or investors (e.g. Steve Blank, Paul Graham, Alexander Osterwalder, Bill Aulet, Eric Ries)—are invited by leading American universities (e.g. Stanford, Harvard, MIT) to co-create education programmes for startup entrepreneurship (this topic will be discussed in more detail in Chap. 3). The opinions of practitioners, although usually unscientific, nevertheless, inspire researchers to study startups and are still the first to point out the most important issues, processes, and problems related to startups. Practitioners' publications, de facto popular science works, commonly recognised in the startup environment as fundamental, will therefore be included in the analysis, despite their lack of methodological rigour, and two of them will be presented in the first place.

The most popular definition of a startup, widely cited not only in industry publications, but also in scientific literature, was formulated by Steve Blank. Blank is a Silicon Valley entrepreneur, and one of the three creators of the *Lean Startup* management concept. He is also an academic—an associate professor of entrepreneurship at Stanford University and a teacher at the prestigious American universities: Berkeley, Columbia, and Caltech. In his works he frequently stated that "a startup is a temporary organisation formed to search for a repeatable and scalable business model" (Blank 2003, 2013). Blank claims that "a startup is not a small version of a large company" (2013) and that startups can be identified by their:

- goals (intentions) that are very ambitious and aim towards becoming a large company that will have a significant impact on the functioning of existing markets or will create entirely new markets;
- function, which, consistently with the definition quoted above, is a search for a business model, which in practice means continuous testing of business hypotheses, their verification, and possible modification of subsequent versions of the business model;
- a financing structure that at the advanced stage of development includes funds obtained from external investors and results in a decreasing share of the founders in the company's capital.

Interestingly, Blank's definition does not include the words "new", "innovative", or "technological". In other words, he doesn't specify the industry, company's age, or product innovation. He does, however, focus on the ambitions and dynamics of business development and, at a later stage, the external sources of funding. The most important element that distinguishes a startup from other undertakings is the "search", which results primarily from the uncertainty as to the demand and the shape of the proposed solution. "Temporary organisation" means any form of achieving a common goal, also within a large company or a corporation (cf. Leten and Van Dyck 2012). The technological element, however, appears implicitly, because the scalability of the business model can be achieved mainly thanks to the automation of important operations (tasks), which ultimately means their algorithmisation and replacement with, for example, a computer programme. For example:

- thanks to one digital platform it is possible to make purchases or order a taxi in an infinite number of cities and countries in the world (eBay, Amazon, Uber);
- a Polish startup Automater.pl has automated the process of sending virtual products sold via online auctions (it records and books payments and immediately sends the customer the purchased product, e.g. a top-up for a mobile phone), that is, the tasks that the sellers used to perform manually.

Summing up Blank's concept, it can be stated that the key features of a startup include searching for a business model (i.e. uncertainty as to the demand and the shape of the offered solution) and, ultimately, the scalability of the enterprise achieved thanks to the use of ICT.

Another widespread definition, often treated as supplementary to Blank's definition, comes from Eric Ries (2011), an entrepreneur-in-residence at the Harvard Business School. He believes that a startup is "a human institution, founded to create a new product or service in the conditions of extreme uncertainty". Ries therefore emphasises startups focusing on the product and the extreme risk in which such organisations operate.

Clayton Christensen, a professor at Harvard Business School and one of the visionaries of innovative entrepreneurship, presented in his famous book *The Innovator's Dilemma* (1997) and many subsequent scientific publications (Christensen and Overdorf 2000; Dyer et al. 2011;

Christensen and Raynor 2013) the concept of the so-called disruptive innovation. In his numerous works, Christensen sees startups as organisations that create breakthrough innovations, that is, organisations which, in the long run, can change market paradigms. The common denominator of academic startup definitions is frequent references to the resources of the company. An expert on financial valuation of companies, a professor at the University of New York, Aswath Damodaran (2009) points to the specific feature of startups, which, according to him, is a high potential for growth in the company's value in the future. Among the secondary characteristics of startups, Damodaran mentions early stage of development, lack of history (also financial history), strong dependence on the sources of capital, and relatively low survival rates. Noam Wasserman (2012), a professor at Harvard Business School, claims that a startup is an organisation that follows market opportunity regardless of the size of its resources. Omar Mohout (Mohout and Kiemen 2016), professor of entrepreneurship at Management School in Antwerp, points to hyper-scalability as a necessary and distinctive startup characteristic. Scalability means that rapidly growing sales do not result in the need to increase human resources in the startup. In other words, a startup is an organisation in which a small team is able to handle thousands, and even millions, of customers.

It is worth noting here that the leading scientific sources are still dominated by the original understanding of a startup as an enterprise in its early stages, a new company. This is evident from the example of the *Web of Science Core Collection* database. The top ten cited articles in the "management" or "business" sections with the word "startup" (or "start-up") as their topic were compiled using that database and are presented in Table 1.2, together with their connotation of the term "startup", broken down into three sets: papers published since 2010, those published since 2013 (i.e. after the publication of Blank's article on "Lean Startup" in *Harvard Business Review*: Blank 2013) and, additionally, those which have the word "startup" in the title as well as in the topic.

In Table 1.2 papers in which "startup" is understood differently than a "new" or "beginner" company/enterprise and which refer to the features associated with knowledge, high technology, and development are marked in bold. This category amounts to three items in the articles published since 2010, two since 2013 and the most, that is, half, in articles since 2013 with the word "startup" in the title. It can thus be confirmed that, in the leading scientific literature, the original understanding of a startup as a beginner enterprise, a new company, still prevails, although publications

Table 1.2 Understanding the concept of "startup" in the ten most cited articles with "startup" as a topic, based on the Web of Science Core Collection

No.	*Published since 2010*	*Published since 2013*	
			and has the word "startup" in the title
1	Ostrom et al. (2010): Company in its early stages of development	Mollick, E. (2014): Cultural or artistic commercial project	*Blank, S.* (2013): *Temporary organisation searching for a scalable business model*
2	Mollick, E. (2014): Cultural or artistic commercial project	Schlaegel and Koenig (2014): Company in its early stages of development	Román et al. (2013): New project
3	Liñán et al. (2011): New company	*Blank, S.* (2013): *Temporary organisation searching for a scalable business model*	Cassar, G. (2014): New project
4	Schlaegel and Koenig (2014): Company in its early stages of development	Kautonen et al. (2015): New company	*Conti et al.* (2013): *Business in the high-tech industry*
5	*Cumming et al.* (2010): *Company co-financed by VC*	Cavusgil and Knight (2015): Young company	Semrau and Werner (2014): New business
6	*Blank, S.* (2013): *Temporary organisation searching for a scalable business model*	Klotz et al. (2014): New company	*Harms, R.* (2015): *Enterprise built on the basis of the Lean Startup methodology*
7	Townsend et al. (2010): New project	*Audretsch* (2014): *A new knowledge-based company*	*Criaco et al.* (2014): *Technology company founded at a university*
8	*Ceccagnoli et al.* (2012): *Small independent software companies*	Liñán and Fayolle (2015): New company	Hyytinen et al. (2015): New company
9	Kautonen et al. (2015): New company	Coad et al. (2013): New company	*Guerrero and Urbano* (2014): *Company* founded *at a university*

(*continued*)

Table 1.2 (continued)

No.	*Published since 2010*	*Published since 2013*	
			and has the word "startup" in the title
10	Liñán et al. (2011): New company	Hoogendoorn et al. (2013): New company	Pe'er and Keil (2013): New company

Source: Own material

sharing the approach presented in this work are appearing increasingly more often. Such ambiguous understanding of the concept of startup may result in significant misunderstandings. If conclusions from "startups" research are compared with each other without a prior reflection about what the researcher considered to be a startup, the results of the analysis will be misleading or even false (cf. Santisteban and Mauricio 2017).

It is worth mentioning a few other definitions or descriptions of the term "startup". Probably the most concise definition (though ambiguous and metaphorical rather than methodological), popular among entrepreneurs, is attributed to Paul Graham, a co-founder of YCombinator, considered to be the best startup accelerator (Airbnb and Dropbox as well as the Polish startup Estimote all developed their business models during acceleration at YCombinator). Graham stated: "startup is growth"; that is, he considered startups to be projects that develop extremely fast and are scalable. This development can mean a rapid increase both in revenues and in the number of users (customers) and, ultimately, the company's value. All other features that characterise startups are, in Graham's opinion, a derivative of the primary function of rapid development.

It is also worth quoting the statements of two well-known and respected investors in the startup environment: Peter Thiel, a co-founder and a former CEO of PayPal, said that "a company is a startup as long as it creates new solutions", which makes the concept extremely broad while emphasising innovation and pioneering solutions. In turn, the previously quoted Marc Andreessen refers to Blank's definition, specifying that a startup searches for a perfect product-market fit.

Publications from business environment institutions and European literature don't add much to the startup definitions presented so far. However, certain definitions with a focus on a more practical and less philosophical dimension have appeared (often intentionally formulated in this way). According to the Global Entrepreneurship Monitor (2016), startups are enterprises which are in the preparation stage and those that already exist, but are managed only by the founders. In turn, the European Commission clearly interprets startups through the prism of industry, stating that a startup is an entity operating in the field of technology entrepreneurship, on the digital market, offering services in the field of web services and ICT. According to the Kauffman Foundation (Fairlie et al. 2015) reports, startups can be identified with *IDEs: Innovation-Driven Enterprises.* but the Foundation also applies, in its other works, a definition according to which a startup is any business that employs at least one person apart from the owner and has been operating for no longer than one year. In its latest publication on startups OECD (Breschi et al. 2018) draws attention to the ambiguity of the definition of a startup (p. 9), and defines a startup as an innovative technological company attempting to face the most difficult civilisational challenges (such as new energy sources, social exclusion, sustainable development).

A Polish Agency for Enterprise Development—PARP—defines a startup in its latest competition documents as “a micro and small enterprise which is a company registered in Poland, not listed on the stock exchange for up to five years after the registration, which has not yet carried out a profit sharing and was not created as a result of a merger” (PARP 2016). On the other hand, on its website, the same agency defines the conditions that must be met by a company to be eligible for “startup support”: (the company must) “be a micro, small or medium entrepreneur, running a business in the Republic of Poland for no longer than three years and be at the stage of signing an investment agreement ”.

Polish literature on the subject also contains attempts to develop original or derivative startup definitions. Jan Antoszkiewicz (2013, p. 12) approached the issue creatively, stating directly that a startup is “a new form for preparing and introducing a new company into economic circulation”. Beata Glinka and Jacek Pasieczny (2015) refer to Blank’s definition, clearly indicating that a startup is a young company. Jerzy Cieślik (2014a, b) points to technology companies operating in the ICT and Internet industries, especially those developed with the goal of a sale to larger market players. Krzysztof Łuczak (2014) considers the features related to the early stage of development, innovation, and growth potential as important, as well as, following Blank, the search for the optimal business model. Agata Gemzik-Salwach (2014) emphasises innovation and the creation of demand, the connection with new technologies, and high levels of risk. Leszek Bursiak (2013) suggests a five-year time limit and private external funding. Finally, Paweł Konopka and Ewa Roszkowska (2015) focus on the lack of operational history, and Dominika Latusek-Jurczak (2017) on rapid growth and scalability. Importantly, in many Polish publications a clear tendency can be observed that although in the introduction to the analysis, startups are discussed as manifestations of innovative, dynamic, and technological entrepreneurship, in the part discussing research, whether own or others, the researchers are forced to use a simplified concept of a "startup" as a new, newly established (registered), enterprise (business).

Based on the analysis, it can be concluded that there are four main features that distinguish startups from other enterprises (Table 1.3):

- the young age of the enterprise and its limited resources (startups are young companies with limited resources, especially financial ones),
- innovation (startups offer innovative solutions in an innovative way),
- development and scalability (startups are ambitious and fast-growing companies),
- the industry in which they operate (startups are companies operating in the digital industry, ICT, or, more broadly, technology companies).

Table 1.3 presents all literature sources discussed earlier, depending on which startup features were considered to be the key ones. Additionally, it also takes into account the authorship of the definition, that is, whether it was proposed by entrepreneurs or investors, scientists, or business environment institutions.

The compilation of key startup features in Table 1.3 shows the discrepancy in the understanding of key startup features that exist between the world of science and business. In the former, the criteria of time and limited resources definitely dominate, while practitioners' definitions do not refer to this element at all, focusing on innovation and developmental dynamism. The existence of such a far-reaching dichotomy is not conducive to cooperation or developing the knowledge about this important economic phenomenon.

Table 1.3 Key startup features according to the discussed definitions

Startup features	*Practitioners: entrepreneurs or investors*	*Scientists*	*Institutions*
Period of operation and resources		Damodaran (2009) Glinka and Pasieczny (2015) Łuczak (2014) Gemzik-Salwach (2014) Bursiak (2013) Konopka and Roszkowska (2015) Ostrom et al. (2010) Schlaegel and Koenig (2014) Román et al. (2013) Liñán et al. (2011) Cassar (2014) Kautonen et al. (2015) Semrau and Werner (2014) Cavusgil and Knight (2015) Cumming et al. (2010) Klotz et al. (2014) Townsend et al. (2010) Liñán and Fayolle (2015) Hyytinen et al. (2015) Coad et al. (2013) Pe'er and Keil (2013) Hoogendoorn et al. (2013)	GEM (2016) PARP (2016)

(*continued*)

Table 1.3 (continued)

Startup features	*Practitioners: entrepreneurs or investors*	*Scientists*	*Institutions*
Innovation	Ries (2011) Thiel and Masters (2014) Andreessen (2007)	Christensen (1997) Wasserman (2012) Antoszkiewicz (2013) Glinka and Pasieczny (2015) Gemzik-Salwach (2014) Audretsch (2014)	Kauffman Foundation (Fairlie et al. 2015) OECD (Breschi et al. 2018)
Development and scalability	Blank (2013) Graham (2012)	Mohout and Kiemen (2016) Łuczak (2014) Cieślik (2014a, b) Latusek-Jurczak (2017) Harms (2015)	OECD (Breschi et al. 2018)
Industry		Cieślik (2017, 2014a, b) Mollick (2014) Conti et al. (2013) Criaco et al. (2014) Ceccagnoli et al. (2012) Guerrero and Urbano (2014)	European Commission (2014)

Source: Own material

1.4 Startup Definition: A Discussion

Considering the definition of a startup, one can also approach the issue *à rebours*, that is, to start with a different question: What is *not* a startup? Following Blank (2013), it should be stated that a company that operates a proven business model, that is, one adopted to minimise the risk of failure, is not a startup. Thus, neither a business setup in a franchise system, nor a proverbial greengrocer's stall, nor any form of traditional trade is a startup. On further consideration, this condition means that a startup must implement some form of innovation—not necessarily an innovative product, but certainly one that means that the answers to the fundamental questions of *what is the product? who is the customer? how to make money from this?* are not obvious and have to be verified under market conditions. Ries (2011) goes further and underlines the necessity for product novelty (innovation). Christensen additionally requires that the innovation implemented by a startup should be of a disruptive nature, that is, radically changing the market status quo. Thus, enterprises that operate using agency formulas or imitate existing solutions are excluded from the set of startups. The breakthrough character of the new solution implemented by a startup results, according to Mohout and Kiemen (2016), in hyper-scalability, that is, an extremely fast increase in sales or the number of users, ultimately leading (after Damodaran 2009) to a very high company valuation. This means that a company that meets the conditions specified above, but does not acquire customers quickly enough to rapidly increase in value, is not a startup either.

Thus, remaining for too long at the stage of a market experiment as well as stable or slowly increasing revenues also characterise *not startups.* A rapidly growing workforce and/or organisational expansion also do not characterise startups, which by their nature should be micro or small companies, managed by their founders, not by hired managerial staff. It can therefore be assumed that when a startup hires such specialists, it ceases to be a startup. Taking into account additional conditions, companies that do not operate in markets related to information processing and are funded from own resources only are not startups either. It is also worth remembering the basic condition that a startup is a new enterprise, a new entrant on the market, with no more than a few years' tenure. The lack of emphasis on projects relying on high-tech solutions in the discussed definitions is somewhat surprising, because, intuitively, such projects are widely considered to be startups.

On this basis, a model of a startup's development together with the growth factors significant at different stages can be proposed. The starting point of a startup's development is knowledge and access to technology. The value of the knowledge is determined by the composition and social capital of the founding team, which is the startup's basic resource at the initial stage of its development. On this basis, a product, or, rather, a value proposition for potential customers is created. If the team has, at this stage, sufficient operational efficiency, that is, the ability to bring business ideas to life, it has a chance to design and verify a business model. If this model starts operating under favourable market conditions, that is, increasing demand and limited competition, it will generate a growing, preferably rapidly growing, number of customers. Ensuring an appropriate level of funding needed to maintain the pace of the development, while also maintaining the quality of production, results in an increase in the value of the entire company, which will benefit its shareholders.

Using the knowledge about startups and the various paths of their development, one can construct a model history of a startup's development. A new company (organisation), with no operational history, tests an innovative business model in conditions of high risk and low, often not consciously realised, demand. The main resource at its disposal is the combination of the knowledge, skills, experience, and social capital of the founders. The core of the new business model is an innovative product or service that results from the application of knowledge and technology, whose breakthrough character and skilful implementation result in creating a disruptive situation on the market. This situation generates an opportunity for hyper-scaling of the business model—provided that the demand barriers are overcome. If this happens, the company grows very rapidly, first in terms of the number of users, then the number of paying customers, and, finally, the value of the company also greatly increases. This growth is usually additionally conditional on a significant increase in the company's capital (from external sources) in order to service rapidly multiplying technical, organisational, and business processes at the stage of dynamic scaling. However, this does not necessarily mean a significant increase in the workforce—especially in the area of operational activities which in a startup aim for automation. In addition, a startup, even organisationally developed, retains its flat and flexible (network) structure, while strong leadership is an important element of its organisational culture.

1.5 Spiral Definition of a Startup

On the basis of the conclusions from the analysis of the definitions and startup growth factors, the author derived her own, original and universal, definition of a startup, called "a spiral definition of a startup". The reference to the spiral shape reflects the idea from the definition which narrows the breadth of the concept of a startup in line with the organisation's maturing. It results from the conviction that the most important criteria identifying startups are different, depending on the stage of the company's development.

The starting point for the spiral definition is therefore the division of the startup life cycle into three basic stages: initial, expansion, and maturity. In the initial phase, a startup is an organisation with limited resources which identifies a market problem, recognises demand, or verifies its solution; at the expansion stage, it is an organisation that grows rapidly (even at double-digit rates per month); and at the maturity stage it is a hyper-scalable organisation. As a result of the definition understood in this way, the population of startups will be numerous in the initial phase and small in the mature phase. Graphically, this definition is well illustrated by the Fibonacci sequence spiral, where the spiralling curve symbolises the path of startup development, the subsequent squares reflect the main features typical of the various stages of the development, and the areas of these squares reflect the decreasing population size (Fig. 1.2).

The spiral definition of a startup is intended primarily as a tool for identifying startups, so its concept and application will be discussed from this perspective.

From a set of all entities entering the market, those characterised by an innovative and unverified business model are selected. In other words, these are organisations that describe the demand for their solution as uncertain, unknown, or even non-existent. In this way, entities with an obviously non-innovative character are eliminated from the startups' population. Of course, the terms "uncertain" or "unknown" are not unambiguous and can be interpreted in various ways, but it is about not trying to duplicate existing, established business models in which no element of the customer-problem-solution triad bears the marks of novelty. Thus, projects that reinterpret, imitate, or simply copy existing solutions are excluded. It is sufficient, however, for at least one element in this triad to be new—it can then be considered that the demand is not obvious. Therefore, solving known problems using a known solution but offered to

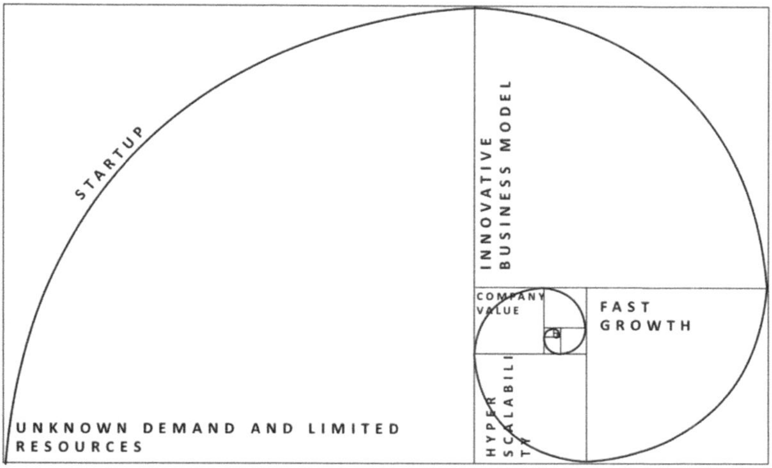

Fig. 1.2 Spiral definition of a startup. (Source: Own material)

a completely new customer segment is an innovative project and so is a known customer and a known problem, but solved in a completely new way. However, someone who creates a new business based on a franchise does not create a startup. A typical store or a sales operation (also online) is not a startup either, as long as it does not utilise new, innovative solutions.

The second condition that must be met by a startup at the initial stage of development is limited and insufficient resources, especially financial ones. In other words there are no "rich" startups—the lack is an immanent feature of this type of organisation.

A startup which has verified its innovative business model moves into the expansion phase. At this stage, the pace of development matters the most—there are no "slow" startups. Therefore, the growth dynamic of revenues or the number of users (customers) is a criterion for identifying startups at this stage.

During a discussion about the definition of a startup, one question is often asked: can a mature organisation be a startup? As part of the spiral definition of a startup, it is assumed that the defining feature of a mature startup is hyper-scalability, understood as a very high ratio of the number of customers or the income generated to the number of employees in a startup. The high market value of the company is also not without significance, calculated mostly at the times of subsequent rounds of external financing. A significant group of startups creates and implements innovations based on new technologies, especially in the broadly understood area of information processing. Hyper-scalability is then achieved through the use of appropriate technology, not by increasing the workforce. It is about finding a global market niche in which the needs can be met by algorithmisation and automation of key tasks. Disruption phenomena often occur at this stage, resulting in the overturning of the market status quo and the development of new consumer habits on a large scale. Thanks to this, startups achieve a rapid growth—first in the number of users (customers), then in the revenues, and, finally, in the company's value. Maintaining such a situation for a long time is very difficult and rare; it is the domain of the largest players on the market—Facebook, Snapchat, Airbnb, and so on—but even their position can be at any time threatened by new solutions that constantly appear on the market.

The term "startup" can also be understood sensu *largo*—as a philosophy of doing business. In this sense, a mature company that remains entrepreneurially "alert", despite the fact that it is operating a proven business model, can also behave like a startup, because it is constantly looking for new opportunities and chances to create and exploit a potentially disruptive situation on the market. It is possible that maintaining such alertness within large, financially stable organisations is even more difficult than developing a classic micro-startup, which is indicated by the fact that few large companies behave in this way, and even fewer do it consistently and for a long time. The example of Apple allows us to presume that maintaining a startup culture in an organisation is closely related to the strength of its leadership (Blank 2016). The example of Microsoft proves, in turn, that a startup character can be both lost and recovered (Gawer and Cusumano 2014).

Few startups reach the "core" of the spiral (among Polish startups, Brainly, znanylekarz.pl, Brand24, Audioteka, and LiveChat can be mentioned). Most of them "fall out" of the spiral, for example, transforming into other organisations: micro-enterprises, medium-sized enterprises, corporations, and non-profit foundations (Fig. 1.3). There are also startups that simply do not find an effective revenue model despite all other conditions being met. Others remain startups for much longer, deciding to operate in an extremely volatile and uncertain market environment.

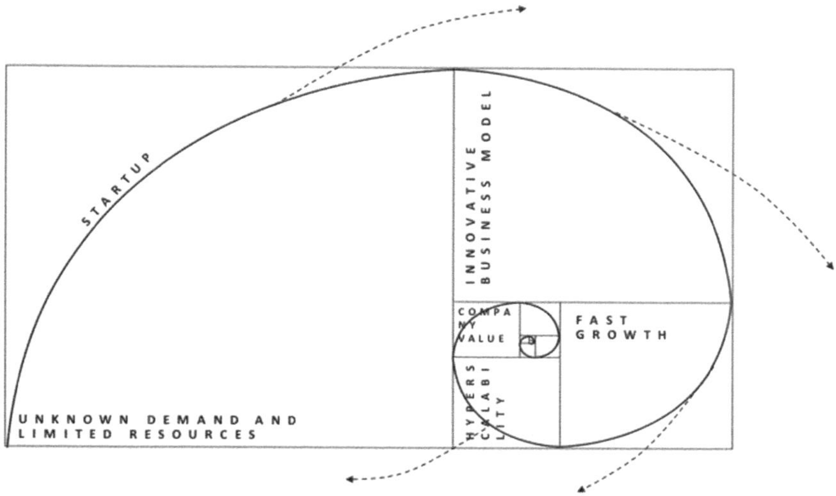

Fig. 1.3 "Falling out" of the startup spiral. (Source: Own material)

The mechanism of falling out of the spiral of the startup definition is one of the most promising directions for further research on startups. The following examples demonstrate the existence of this phenomenon:

- transforming a startup into a foundation: the "Geek Girls Carrots" initiative was a startup at the beginning of its operation, because it was not clear how much the idea of increasing women's participation in the IT and programmers' community would find supporters among the potential participants, but it did not have any meaningful resources and it was also not known on what basis this activity should be organised (a business model was sought); currently (2018) "Geek Girls Carrots" is a mature, global non-profit organisation, stable and functioning within a verified and repeatable business model;
- transforming a startup into a corporation: Onet.pl (created by the merger of Optimus-Net and Optimus Pascal) was the first Polish Internet portal (founded in 1996) which transformed into a powerful player on the media market, whose main shareholder is the global potentate Ringier Axel Springer Media AG, with the TVN Group as a minority shareholder;

- sale of a startup: the HumanWay recruitment tool was sold to Grupa Pracuj at the stage of rapid growth, and the Gastronauci.pl portal to the Indian company Zomato;
- dismantling of a startup: the development of the promising startup MyGuid.ie (Myguidie) was halted after one year of operation due to its failing to implement a viable business model.

Based on the observation of startups, one can also formulate the thesis that in certain situations the reasons for falling out of the spiral may be of a more psychological than business nature: the founders sometimes lack faith, energy, and ambition to start or continue functioning in a startup mode and stop at reaching a stage of development that is satisfactory for them. The following typology of such entrepreneurs can be proposed here:

- a supporter of safe business, who after identifying a suitable target group and providing basic resources for an innovative enterprise is not interested in further development (so-called koala bear);
- an entrepreneur without a bold vision of the future, who is satisfied with finding an innovative business model, but decides not to expand (so-called Winnie the Pooh);
- retreating from the battle, when the entrepreneur succumbs to doubts about the success or own abilities at the stage of the rapid growth; or the resources accumulated by the team are actually too weak to support the high rate of development (so-called crab);
- settling on laurels, when the entrepreneur withdraws at the stage of hyper-scalability, satisfied with the level of development that has already been achieved (so-called sybarite)

A process that is opposite to "falling out", that is, "falling into" the startup spiral, can also be observed in projects that were not originally created as startups. For example, a company operating in the agency model (acting each time on customers' commission) starts developing its own specific product and searches for a broad target group; for example, the Hanbright interactive agency has evolved into the ciufcia.pl startup, and ultimately into Duckie Deck. Another company providing various robotic solutions for different clients begins to focus on a specific product as its internal project (a startup)—a robot for the construction industry. In both cases, the company is not sure which mode of its operations (on-commission or product-oriented) will be the ultimate one.

As mentioned earlier, an examination of the definitions of a startup was motivated by the need to develop a method for identifying these organisations among other enterprises. Figure 1.4 thus presents the algorithm for identifying startups based on the spiral definition of a startup.

The algorithm presented in Fig. 1.4 will be used for in-depth analysis of startups which participated in the nationwide "Polish Startups" study, and whose results will be presented in Chap. 2.

1.6 Chapter Summary

The analysis presented in this chapter aimed to answer the question of what a startup is and what features distinguish it from other organisations. A startup is an agent of innovation, especially the latest achievements of science and technology, allowing the economies of developed countries, exhausted by the financial crisis, to regain their "fresh breath". That's why understanding what a startup is and how it operates should be of interest to state institutions, regional authorities, corporations, research institutes,

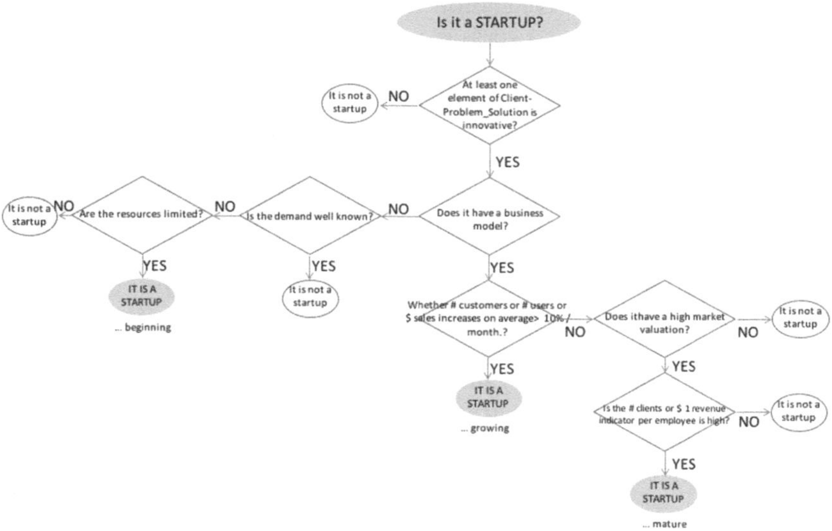

Fig. 1.4 The algorithm for identifying a startup based on the spiral definition of a startup. (Source: Own material)

universities, and other participants in the broadly understood ecosystem of innovative entrepreneurship.

Steve Blank, the author of the most popular definition of a startup so far, defined it as a temporary, and therefore ephemeral, organisation which after some time, having fulfilled its role, is transformed into something else. This does not mean that the effects of its operation are ephemeral, as startups ultimately turn into dynamic companies with high market valuation and a very high number of customers and/or high revenues.

The analysis of literature, supplemented by the author's own consideration and the practical knowledge of the operation of the study subject, allows for the examination and understanding of the startup phenomenon as an economic phenomenon. The chapter has presented the main definitions (or, rather, commonly used terms) for a startup, formulated in the following communities: academics, entrepreneurs, investors, and business environment institutions. A startup development model has been proposed, the main startup growth factors have been indicated, and the concept of the spiral definition of a startup and the startup identification algorithm created on its basis have been presented. Thus, the research goal of this chapter has been accomplished.

The most important conclusion from this chapter's considerations is that the features defining a startup are different for projects in the initial stages of development and for mature organisations. Whereas at the beginning of functioning the key features of a startup are innovation, unknown demand, and limited internal resources, a startup at the advanced stage of its development is an enterprise that exploits market-disruptive situations, which allows it to achieve hyper-scalability and a high company valuation. The intermediate stage in the development of a startup is described by an above-average rate of growth of key company parameters: the number of customers (users) or the revenues. Many startups transform, over time, into other organisations: small or medium-sized companies, corporations, foundations, and so on.

The main features of an organisation that is a startup can also be divided into external and internal factors. The former include initially uncertain demand, a chance for a disruptive market situation, and the possibility of obtaining significant financing at the stage of advanced development. The latter include very limited resources at the beginning, a high operational capacity of the team for testing business models, and strong leadership. A key feature of mature startups is hyper-scalability, which a startup can achieve through appropriate utilisation of technologies that automate repetitive tasks or activities. That's why a special feature of startups is the use of advanced digital technologies in their operations, especially those related to broadly understood information processing.

The population of startups will be, by default, more numerous in the group of beginner enterprises. Only some of them will remain startups on reaching maturity. Some of them will simply fail; others will develop into various other forms of activity, losing their pure startup character: they will become corporations (like Onet.pl and Allegro), medium or large companies (like Audioteka or Netguru), or will be taken over by large players (e.g. Filmaster).

The concept of a "startup" can also be understood as a philosophy of doing business. In this sense, companies such as Google or Facebook are still startups, even though they have evolved into powerful global corporations. However, they are still characterised by particularly intense entrepreneurial alertness and they still set the trends in their industry. They are also the source of the best talent supplying startup ecosystems.

Based on the observations made, one may also put forward the thesis that a significant role in startup development is played by a specific startup culture, strong leadership, and widespread mechanisms for sharing knowledge and experiences within local centres ("hubs"), where startup density increases, creating communities referred to as ecosystems. This thread will be further developed in Chap. 2.

References

Ács, Z. J., & Audretsch, D. B. (1988). Innovation in large and small firms: An empirical analysis. *The American Economic Review, 78*(4), 678–690.

Ács, Z. J., & Audretsch, D. B. (1990). *Innovation and small firms.* Cambridge, MA: MIT Press.

Ács, Z. J., Braunerhjelm, P., Audretsch, D. B., & Carlsson, B. (2009). The knowledge spillover theory of entrepreneurship. *Small Business Economics, 32*(1), 15–30.

Alexy, O. T., Block, J. H., Sandner, P., & Ter Wal, A. L. (2012). Social capital of venture capitalists and start-up funding. *Small Business Economics, 39*(4), 835–851.

Andreessen, M. (2007). The only thing that matters. http://pmarchive.com/guide_to_startups_part4.html. Accessed 17 Jan 2017.

Andreessen, M. (2011). Why software is eating the world. *Wall Street Journal, 20,* C2.

Andrews, D., Criscuolo, C., & Menon, C. (2014). *Do resources flow to patenting firms? Cross-country evidence from firm level data* (OECD Economic Development Department Working Papers, vol. 1127). OECD: Paris.

Antoszkiewicz, J. D. (2013). Rola formułowania wizji i misji w zależności od sytuacji rynkowej dla dużych biznesowych organizacji oraz start-upów. *Przedsiębiorczość i Zarządzanie, XIV*(8), Wydawnictwo SAN, part II, 9–23.

Audretsch, D. B. (2014). From the entrepreneurial university to the university for the entrepreneurial society. *The Journal of Technology Transfer, 39*(3), 313–321.

Audretsch, D. B., & Keilbach, M. (2004). Entrepreneurship capital and economic performance. *Regional Studies, 38*(8), 949–959.

Baptista, R., & Swann, P. (1998). Do firms in clusters innovate more? *Research Policy, 27*(5), 525–540.

Baumol, W. J. (1990). Entrepreneurship: Productive, unproductive, and destructive. *Journal of Political Economy, 98*(5), 893–921.

Baumol, W. J. (2010). *The microtheory of the innovative entrepreneur*. Princeton/Oxford: Princeton University Press.

Bertoni, F., & Tykvová, T. (2015). Does governmental venture capital spur invention and innovation? Evidence from young European biotech companies. *Research Policy, 44*(4), 925–935.

Birch, D. L. (1979). *The job generation process, MIT program on neighborhood and regional change*. Cambridge, MA: MIT Program on Neighborhood and regional Change.

Birch, D. L. (1987). *Job creation in America: How our smallest companies put the most people to work*. New York: The Free Press.

Blanchenay, P. F., Calvino, C., Criscuolo, C., & Menon, C. (2017). *Cross-country evidence on business dynamics over the last decade: From boom to gloom?* (Working Paper). OECD Science, Technology and Industry.

Blank, S. (2003). *The four steps to the epiphany: Successful strategies for products that win*. Pescadero: K&S Ranch.

Blank, S. (2013). Why the lean start-up changes everything. *Harvard Business Review, 91*(5), 63–72.

Blank, S. (2016). Why visionary CEOs never have visionary successors. *Harvard Business Review*. http://hbr.org/2016/10/why-visionary-ceos-never-have-visionary-successors. Accessed 17 Jan 2017.

Block, J. H., Fisch, C. O., Hahn, A., & Sandner, P. G. (2015). Why do SMEs le trademarks? Insights from firms in innovative industries. *Research Policy, 44*(10), 1915–1930.

Block, J. H., Fisch, C. O., & van Praag, M. (2017). The Schumpeterian entrepreneur: A review of the empirical evidence on the antecedents, behaviour and consequences of innovative entrepreneurship. *Industry and Innovation, 24*(1), 61–95.

Borowiecki, R., & Dziura, M. (2016). Nowa gospodarka – aspekty wiedzy i innowacji. *Przegląd Organizacji, 5*, 9–16.

Brem, A., & Voigt, K.-I. (2009). Integration of market pull and technology push in the corporate front end and innovation management – Insights from the German software industry. *Technovation, 29*(5), 351–367.

Breschi, S. J., Lassébie, C., & Menon, C. (2018). *A portrait of innovative start-ups across countries* (OECD Science, Technology and Industry Working Papers). OECD.

Burgelman, R. A., & Sayles, L. R. (1988). *Inside corporate innovation*. New York: Simon and Schuster.

Bursiak, L. (2013). Diagnoza i pozycjonowanie sytuacji nansowej firm start-up oraz spółek z rynku New-Connect w roku 2011. *Zeszyty Naukowe Uniwersytetu Szczecińskiego. Finanse. Rynki nansowe. Ubezpieczenia, 760*(59), 49–58.

Calvino, F. C., Criscuolo, C., & Menon, C. (2016). *No country for young firms?: Start-up dynamics and national policies* (OECD Science, Technology and Industry Policy Papers no 29). OECD Publishing, Paris.

Cantillon, R. (1755). *Essai sur la nature du commerce* (H. Higgs, Trans.). London: Macmillan.

Carree, M. A., & Thurik, A. R. (2008). The lag structure of the impact of business ownership on economic performance in OECD countries. *Small Business Economics, 30*(1), 101–110.

Cassar, G. (2014). Industry and startup experience on entrepreneur forecast performance in new firms. *Journal of Business Venturing, 29*(1), 137–151.

Cavusgil, S. T., & Knight, G. (2015). The born global firm: An entrepreneurial and capabilities perspective on early and rapid internationalization. *Journal of International Business Studies, 46*(1), 3–16.

Ceccagnoli, M., Forman, C., Huang, P., & Wu, D. J. (2012). Cocreation of value in a platform ecosystem! The case of enterprise software. *MIS Quarterly, 36*(1), 263–290.

Christensen, C. (1997). *The innovator's dilemma: When new technologies cause great firms to fail*. Boston: Harvard Business School Press.

Christensen, C., & Bower, J. L. (1996). Customer power, strategic investment, and the failure of leading firms. *Boston Strategic Management Journal, 17*(3), 197–218.

Christensen, C., & Overdorf, M. (2000). Meeting the challenge of disruptive change. *Harvard Business Review, 78*(2), 66–77.

Christensen, C., & Raynor, M. (2013). *The innovator's solution: Creating and sustaining successful growth*. Boston: Harvard Business Review Press.

Ciechanowski, L., Przegalińska, A., & Wegner, K. (2018). The necessity of new paradigms in measuring human-chatbot interaction. In M. Hoffman (Ed.), *Advances in cross-cultural decision making*, AHFE 2017, Advances in Intelligent Systems and Computing, vol. 610. Cham: Springer.

Cieślik, J. (2014a). *Przedsiębiorczość, polityka, rozwój*. Warszawa: Wydawnictwo Akademickie Sedno.

Cieślik, J. (2014b). Iluzje innowacyjnej przedsiębiorczości. *Kwartalnik Nauk o Przedsiębiorstwie, 3*, 4–16.

Cieślik, J. (2017). *Entrepreneurship in emerging economies: Enhancing its contribution to socio-economic development*. Cham: Palgrave Macmillan.

Coad, A., Frankish, J., Roberts, R. G., & Storey, D. J. (2013). Growth paths and survival chances: An application of Gambler's Ruin theory. *Journal of Business Venturing, 28*(5), 615–632.
Cohen, W. M. (1995). Empirical studies of innovative activity. In P. Stoneman (Ed.), *Handbook of the economics of innovation and technological change*. Oxford: Blackwell.
Conti, A., Thursby, M., & Rothaermel, F. T. (2013). Show me the right stuff: Signals for high-tech startups. *Journal of Economics & Management Strategy, 22*(2), 341–364.
Criaco, G., Minola, T., Migliorini, P., & Serarols-Tarrés, C. (2014). "To have and have not": Founders' human capital and university start-up survival. *The Journal of Technology Transfer, 39*(4), 567–593.
Criscuolo, C., Gal, P. N., & Menon, C. (2014). *The dynamics of employment growth: New evidence from 18 countries* (OECD Science, Technology and Industry Policy Papers, nr 14). Paris: OECD Publishing.
Csaszar, F., Nussbaum, M., & Sepulveda, M. (2006). Strategic and cognitive criteria for the selection of startups. *Technovation, 26*(2), 151–161.
Cumming, D., Schmidt, D., & Walz, U. (2010). Legality and venture capital governance around the world. *Journal of Business Venturing, 25*(1), 54–72.
Damodaran, A. (2009). *Valuing young, start-up and growth companies: Estimation issues and valuation challenges*. New York: Stern School of Business, New York University.
Decker, R. A., Haltiwanger, J., Jarmin, R. S., & Miranda, J. (2016). Where has all the skewness gone? The decline in high-growth (young) rms in the US. *European Economic Review, 86*, 4–23.
Dörner, K., & Edelman, D. (2015). *What 'digital' really means*. McKinsey & Company. https://www.mckinsey.com/industries/high-tech/our-insights/what-digital-really-means. Accessed 1 Dec 2017.
Drucker, P. F. (1992). The new society of organizations. *Harvard Business Review, 70*(September–October), 95–104.
Dushnitsky, G., & Lenox, M. J. (2005). When do incumbents learn from entrepreneurial ventures? Corporate venture capital and investing firm innovation rates. *Research Policy, 34*(5), 615–639.
Dyer, J., Gregersen, H., & Christensen, C. M. (2011). *The innovator's DNA: Mastering the five skills of disruptive innovators*. Boston: Harvard Business Press.
Eisenhardt, K. M., & Schoonhoven, C. B. (1996). Resource-based view of strategic alliance formation: Strategic and social effects in entrepreneurial firms. *Organization Science, 7*(2), 136–150.
Elfring, T., & Hulsink, W. (2003). Networks in entrepreneurship: The case of high-technology firms. *Small Business Economics, 21*(4), 409–422.
European Commission. (2014). Startup Europe. http://ec.europa.eu/digital-single-market/en/policies/startup-europe. Accessed 17 Jan 2017.

Fairlie, R. W., Kapur, K., & Gates, S. (2011). Is employer-based health insurance a barrier to entrepreneurship? *Journal of Health Economics, 30*(1), 146–162.
Fairlie, R. W., Morelix, A., Reedy, E. J., & Russell, J. (2015). *The Kauffman Index 2015: Startup activity, national trends.* https://ssrn.com/abstract=2613479. Accessed 17 Jan 2017.
Gans, J. S., & Stern, S. (2003). The product market and the market for 'ideas': Commercialization strategies for technology entrepreneurs. *Research Policy, 32*(2), 333–350.
Gawer, A., & Cusumano, M. A. (2014). Industry platforms and ecosystem innovation. *Journal of Product Innovation Management, 31*(3), 417–433.
Gemzik-Salwach, A. (2014). Wykorzystanie metody Dave'a Berkusa do analizy potencjału rozwojowego firm start-up w Polsce. *Acta Universitatis Lodziensis. Folia Oeconomica, 2*(300), 111–122.
Giones, F., & Brem, A. (2017). Digital technology entrepreneurship: A definition and research agenda. *Technology Innovation Management Review, 7*(5), 44–51.
Giones, F., & Miralles, F. (2015). Do actions matter more than resources? A signalling theory perspective on the technology entrepreneurship process. *Technology Innovation Management Review, 5*(3), 39–45.
Glinka, B., & Pasieczny, J. (2015). *Tworzenie przedsiębiorstwa: szanse, realizacja, rozwój.* Warszawa: Wydawnictwo Naukowe Wydziału Zarządzania Uniwersytetu Warszawskiego.
Global Entrepreneurship Monitor. (2016). *GEM Global Report.* http://gemconsortium.org/report. Accessed 17 Jan 2017.
Graham, P. (2012). Startup = growth, (self-published online article). http://www.paulgraham.com/growth.html. Accessed 17 Jan 2017.
Guerrero, M., & Urbano, D. (2014). Academics' start-up intentions and knowledge filters: An individual perspective of the knowledge spillover theory of entrepreneurship. *Small Business Economics, 43*(1), 57–74.
Guzman, J., & Stern, S. (2016). *The state of American entrepreneurship: New estimates of the quantity and quality of entrepreneurship for 15 US states, 1988–2014* (National Bureau of Economic Research, Working Paper, no 22095).
Haltiwanger, J., Jarmin, R. S., & Miranda, J. (2013). Who creates jobs? Small versus large versus young. *Review of Economics and Statistics, 95*(2), 347–361.
Harms, R. (2015). Self-regulated learning, team learning and project performance in entrepreneurship education: Learning in a lean startup environment. *Technological Forecasting and Social Change, 100*, 21–28.
Henderson, R. (1993). Underinvestment and incompetence as responses to radical innovation – Evidence from the photolithographic alignment equipment industry. *Rand Journal of Economics, 24*(2), 248–270.
Henkel, J., Rønde, T., & Wagner, M. (2015). And the winner is – Acquired. Entrepreneurship as a contest yielding radical innovations. *Research Policy, 44*(2), 295–310.

Henrekson, M., & Sanandaji, T. (2014). Small business activity does not measure entrepreneurship. *Proceedings of the National Academy of Sciences, 111*(5), 1760–1765.

Hofmokl, J. (2009). *Internet jako nowe dobro wspólne*. Warszawa: Wydawnictwa Akademickie i Profesjonalne.

Hoogendoorn, S., Oosterbeek, H., & Van Praag, M. (2013). The impact of gender diversity on the performance of business teams: Evidence from a field experiment. *Management Science, 59*(7), 1514–1528.

Hyytinen, A., Pajarinen, M., & Rouvinen, P. (2015). Does innovativeness reduce startup survival rates? *Journal of Business Venturing, 30*(4), 564–581.

Kautonen, T., Gelderen, M., & Fink, M. (2015). Robustness of the theory of planned behavior in predicting entrepreneurial intentions and actions. *Entrepreneurship Theory and Practice, 39*(3), 655–674.

Klotz, A. C., Hmieleski, K. M., Bradley, B. H., & Busenitz, L. W. (2014). New venture teams: A review of the literature and roadmap for future research. *Journal of Management, 40*(1), 226–255.

Koellinger, P. (2008). Why are some entrepreneurs more innovative than others? *Small Business Economics, 31*, 21–37.

Konopka, P., & Roszkowska, E. (2015). Zastosowanie metody UTA do wspomagania podejmowania decyzji o finansowaniu startupów działalności gospodarczej. *Optimum Studia Ekonomiczne, 3*, 138–153.

Kösters, S. (2010). Subsidizing start-ups: Policy targeting and policy effectiveness. *Journal of Industry, Competition and Trade, 10*(3–4), 199–225.

Latusek-Jurczak, D. (2017). Firmy szybkiego wzrostu w środowisku niskiego zaufania – badanie empiryczne. *Studia Oeconomica Posnaniensia, 5*(9), 37–49.

Lerner, J. (2004). *The new financial thing: The origins of financial innovations*. Boston: Harvard Business School.

Leten, B., & Van Dyck, W. (2012). Corporate venturing: Strategies and success factors. *Review of Business and Economic Literature, 57*(4), 242.

Liñán, F., & Fayolle, A. (2015). A systematic literature review on entrepreneurial intentions: Citation, thematic analyses, and research agenda. *International Entrepreneurship and Management Journal, 11*(4), 907–933.

Liñán, F., Rodriguez-Cohard, J. C., & Rueda-Cantuche, J. M. (2011). Factors affecting entrepreneurial intention levels: A role for education. *International Entrepreneurship and Management Journal, 7*(2), 195–218.

Łuczak, K. (2014). Rachunkowość innowacji na przykładzie przedsiębiorstw określanych mianem start-up. *Zeszyty Naukowe Uniwersytetu Szczecińskiego. Finanse. Rynki finansowe. Ubezpieczenia, 827*(70), 79–87.

Mohout, O., & Kiemen, M. (2016). *A critical perspective to exponential organizations and its hyper scalability*. http://mixel.be/files/pdf/Critical-to-exponential_preprint.pdf. Accessed 17 Jan 2017.

Mollick, E. (2014). The dynamics of crowdfunding: An exploratory study. *Journal of Business Venturing, 29*(1), 1–16.

Nambisan, S. (2016). Digital entrepreneurship: Toward a digital technology perspective of entrepreneurship. *Entrepreneurship Theory and Practice, 414*, 1–27.

Ng, W., & Stuart, T. E. (2016). *Of Hobos and Highfliers: Disentangling the classes and careers of technology-based entrepreneurs* (Working Paper). https://www.gsb.stanford.edu/sites/gsb/les/ng_italk2016_0.pdf. Accessed 20 Feb 2017.

Noga, A. (2009). *Teorie przedsiębiorstw*. Warszawa: PWE.

OECD. (2015). *Entrepreneurship at a glance 2015*. Paris: OECD Publishing.

OECD. (2017). *Business dynamics and productivity*. Paris: OECD Publishing. https://doi.org/10.1787/9789264269231-en

Ostrom, A. L., Bitner, M. J., Brown, S. W., Burkhard, K. A., Goul, M., Smith-Daniels, V., & Rabinovich, E. (2010). Moving forward and making a difference: Research priorities for the science of service. *Journal of Service Research, 13*(1), 4–36.

Paprocki, W. (2016). Koncepcja Przemysł 4.0 i jej zastosowanie w warunkach gospodarki cyfrowej. In J. Pieriegud & W. Paprocki (Eds.), *Cyfryzacja gospodarki i społeczeństwa. Szanse i wyzwania dla sektorów infrastrukturalnych*. Gdańsk: Publikacja Europejskiego Kongresu Finansowego.

PARP. (2016). *Program Operacyjny Inteligentny Rozwój. Scale up*. https://poir.parp.gov.pl/attachments/article/37225/pytania%20i%20odpowiedzi%20scaleup_POIR%20sierpien.pdf. Accessed 17 Jan 2017.

Pe'er, A., & Keil, T. (2013). Are all startups affected similarly by clusters? Agglomeration, competition, firm heterogeneity, and survival. *Journal of Business Venturing, 28*(3), 354–372.

Pieriegud, J. (2016). Cyfryzacja gospodarki i społeczeństwa – wymiar globalny, europejski i krajowy. In J. Pieriegud & W. Paprocki (Eds.), *Cyfryzacja gospodarki i społeczeństwa. Szanse i wyzwania dla sektorów infrastrukturalnych*. Gdańsk: Publikacja Europejskiego Kongresu Finansowego.

Prats, J., Amigó, P., Ametller, X., Batlle, A. (2017). *Corporate venturing: Achieving profitable growth through startups*. Barcelona: mVenturesBcn.

Priem, R. L., Li, S., & Carr, J. C. (2011). Insights and new directions from demand-side approaches to technology innovation, entrepreneurship, and strategic management research. *Journal of Management, 38*(1), 346–374.

Przegalińska, A. (2016). *Fenomenologia istot wirtualnych*. Kraków: TAiWPN Universitas.

Rannikko, H., & Autio, E. (2016). Retaining winners: Can policy boost high-growth entrepreneurship? *Research Policy, 45*(1), 42–55.

Ries, E. (2011). *The lean startup: How today's entrepreneurs use continuous innovation to create radically successful businesses*. New York: Crown Business.

Román, C., Congregado, E., & Millán, J. M. (2013). Start-up incentives: Entrepreneurship policy or active labour market programme? *Journal of Business Venturing, 28*(1), 151–175.

Santisteban, J., & Mauricio, D. (2017). Systematic literature review of critical success factors of information technology startups. *Academy of Entrepreneurship Journal, 23*(2), 1–23.
Say, J.-B. (1841). *Traité d'économie politique: ou simple exposition de la manière dont se forment, se distribuent et se consomment les richesses.* Paris: Guillaumin.
Scherer, F. M. (1984). *Innovation and growth: Schumpeterian perspectives*, Chapter 11. Cambridge, MA: MIT Press.
Schlaegel, C., & Koenig, M. (2014). Determinants of entrepreneurial intent: A meta-analytic test and integration of competing models. *Entrepreneurship Theory and Practice, 38*(2), 291–332.
Schoar, A. (2010). The divide between subsistence and transformational entrepreneurship. *Innovation Policy and the Economy, 10*(1), 57–81.
Schumpeter, J. (1942). *Capitalism, socialism and democracy.* New York: Harper & Brothers.
Semrau, T., & Werner, A. (2014). How exactly do network relationships pay off? The effects of network size and relationship quality on access to start-up resources. *Entrepreneurship Theory and Practice, 38*(3), 501–525.
Shane, S. A. (2000). Prior knowledge and the discovery of entrepreneurial opportunities. *Organization Science, 11*(4), 448–469.
Shane, S. A. (2003). *A general theory of entrepreneurship.* Cheltenham: Edward Elgar.
Shane, S. A. (2008). *The illusions of entrepreneurship: The costly myths that entrepreneurs, investors and policy makers live by.* New Haven: Yale University Press.
Skala, A. (2016). *Start-upy: ambitne i samodzielne.* Rzeczpospolita z 2 sierpnia. http://www.rp.pl/Telekomunikacja-i-IT/308019881-Start-upy-ambitne-i-samodzielne.html. Accessed 31 Jan 2017.
Stępniak-Kucharska, A. (2015). Rola państwa we wspieraniu działalności badawczo-rozwojowej polskich przedsiębiorstw. *Studia Ekonomiczne, 209*, 199–208.
Thiel, P. A., & Masters, B. (2014). *Zero to one: Notes on startups, or how to build the future.* New York: Crown Publishing Group.
Townsend, D. M., Busenitz, L. W., & Arthurs, J. D. (2010). To start or not to start: Outcome and ability expectations in the decision to start a new venture. *Journal of Business Venturing, 25*(2), 192–202.
Utterback, J. M. (1995). *Mastering the dynamics of innovation.* Boston: Harvard Business School Press.
Wasserman, N. (2012). *The founder's dilemmas: Anticipating and avoiding the pitfalls that can sink a startup.* New Jersey: Princeton University Press.
Wennekers, S., & Thurik, R. (1999). Linking entrepreneurship and economic growth. *Small Business Economics, 13*(1), 27–56.
Wojtyna, A. (2001). *Czy tradycyjna ekonomia pozwala zrozumieć nową gospodarkę?* Referat na VII Kongres Ekonomistów Polskich, Warszawa.
Wong, P., Ho, Y., & Autio, E. (2005). Entrepreneurship, innovation and economic growth: Evidence from GEM data. *Small Business Economics, 24*(3), 335–350.

CHAPTER 2

Characteristics of Startups

Abstract This chapter presents selected research on startups undertaken by various organisations worldwide, from the point of view of their comparability and the definitions of the research object they used. A large part of this chapter is devoted to the presentation of a startup research project in Poland, undertaken and coordinated since 2015 by the author in collaboration with the Startup Poland Foundation. Since 2017, the study has also covered the Czech Republic, Slovakia, and Hungary. The description of the preparation, implementation, and analysis of this extensive study can provide guidance for other startup researchers. The results are analysed, which allowed for determining the key factors differentiating the surveyed group of enterprises and for outlining the emerging trends in the area of startups' development directions.

Keywords Own research • "Polish Startups" • Visegrád Group • Characteristics of startups • Differentiating variables

In Chap. 1, it has been demonstrated that in the literature of the subject, the term "startup" is understood in various ways. On the one hand, in the academic community, the dominant approach identifies startups with beginner companies that enter the market with limited resources and little business experience. On the other hand, for entrepreneurs and investors, startups have been understood as highly innovative and dynamically

A. Skala, *Digital Startups in Transition Economies*,
https://doi.org/10.1007/978-3-030-01500-8_2

developing enterprises that utilise digital technologies. This discrepancy hinders the dialogue between theory and business practice, creates conceptual chaos, and means that research on startups generates ambiguous and incomparable results (cf. Santisteban and Mauricio 2017; Breschi et al. 2018). Meanwhile, understanding and describing startups is important in the context of the key role they are to play in the process of revitalising the contemporary economy. Therefore, this chapter aims to provide a description of startups and to identify the features that differentiate them from other business entities. The chapter will also verify the concept of a startup proposed in Chap. 1 in the light of research results. These objectives will be achieved on the basis of a critical analysis of selected startup studies, including:

- secondary data, based on research undertaken worldwide and published by scientists, businesses, and organisations;
- primary research (the "Polish Startups" research project), covering a sample of approximately 2000 startups in Poland between 2015 and 2017, designed and coordinated by the author, and carried out by the Startup Poland Foundation; parts of the project also had a regional dimension and included startups in other Visegrád Group countries (the Czech Republic, Slovakia, and Hungary).

The description of startups will be expanded with a discussion of the growing importance of "startup ecosystems" which, as indicated by the literature analysis and the results of the author's own research, are an inseparable element of the startup organisational culture. The last part of the chapter will be devoted to in-depth segmentation analysis, which will indicate the most important attributes that differentiate startup as a specific form of organisation.

2.1 Desk Research: Literature Review

Every year more and more research centres, consulting companies, and other organisations carry out research on startups. As mentioned earlier, the results of those projects don't amount to a coherent picture, because individual researchers apply their own understanding of the term "startup", rather than a universally accepted definition. Using a startup definition as a grouping criterion, the research publications on this topic may be grouped into three main categories:

- startups understood as beginner companies in the early stages of operation,
- startups understood as new enterprises which commercialise scientific achievements, that is, new-technology-based firms (NTBFs),
- startups understood as entities creating and using (in their core activities) digital technologies (in other words, digital startups, IT, or information and communication technologies [ICT]),

The picture of startups belonging to the first of these groups is particularly diverse (Calvino et al. 2016; Guzman and Stern 2016; Criscuolo et al. 2014; Haltiwanger et al. 2013; Wong et al. 2005) and often suggests a need for in-depth analysis, as the subgroup of innovative and fast-growing enterprises has different attributes than other studied entities (cf. Breschi et al. 2018).

Research on startups understood as NTBFs has a long tradition, in particular with regard to the achievements of researchers from the Manchester Business School circle and Dutch universities, who since 1993 have organised a recurring series of conferences "*High Technology Small Firms*". This output is also partially related to digital industry startups, according to the typology proposed by Giones and Brem (2017), where "digital technologies entrepreneurship" occupies an intersection between technological and digital entrepreneurship. Interestingly, and similarly to startups, there is no consensus regarding an unambiguous definition of NTBFs (cf. Cunha et al. 2013). Originally, they were defined as companies using new advanced technologies or operating in new, fast-growing industries, including IT (Kelley and Nakosteen 2005; Autio 1997; Rothwell 1989; Cooper 1971). The key attributes of such enterprises include high expenditure on research and development (R&D) and the transformation of new technical knowledge into business solutions (Cooper 1971). Cunha et al. (2013) stated, however, that, although "NTBF" was a common term in the literature and appeared to be thoroughly researched, this was illusory, because the definition remained unclear, and its understanding differed significantly between individual authors (e.g. Fontes and Coombs 2001; Storey and Tether 1998; Laranja and Fontes 1998; Autio 1997; Bollinger et al. 1983). This lack of consensus in the conceptualisation of NTBF also makes it impossible to carry out fully comparable research and to develop a comprehensive description of this group of companies.

When it comes to digital startups, the most worthy of mention are academic studies carried out on entities registered in the Crunchbase startups database (see Dalle et al. 2017; Block et al. 2015; Alexy et al. 2012). Crunchbase is a database of innovative enterprises created in 2007, itself initially a startup (Crunchbase Inc.), containing numerous data on technology companies, especially those connected to the IT and ICT sectors. Crunchbase provides information about the company's capital structure, types of products and services provided, founders, employees, transactions, and so on. Crunchbase lists approximately half a million entities from around 200 countries, and a similar number of entrepreneurs; approximately 50,000 investors including private venture capital (VC) funds, business angels (BAs), investment banks, incubators, public funds, and so on; a quarter of a million of VC transactions; and a lot of other data. The data on capital transactions (investments, acquisitions, or Initial Public Offering (IPO)) are mainly provided by the investment funds themselves, as well as numerous individual or institutional content contributors, especially the entrepreneurs themselves. The database is supplemented and updated not only by the analysts and an advanced information retrieval system developed as part of Crunchbase itself, but to a large extent directly by companies' IT lists, using a crowdsourced database model, which makes it highly credible. This is a result of the fact that it is widely known that this database is the basic source of information for investors seeking valuable companies, so developing startups are themselves very interested in ensuring that the database contains up-to-date and true information about them, while entities that enter the market want to be listed there. More than 3000 investment companies update the data on their portfolio companies every month in exchange for a free access to Crunchbase. Access to data is free of charge for academic researchers, and the database is conveniently structured for searching and can be easily combined with other data sources (e.g. with patent databases). Dalle et al. (2017) listed nearly 100 scientific studies completed with the use of Crunchbase data. The newest such study is dated 2018 (Breschi et al. 2018).[1]

With regard to the empirical research on startups in the digital industry, the analysis of the literature reveals a certain discrepancy that can be observed between the world of theory and the world of practice. Research of a strictly scientific nature is neither well known nor popular among

[1]The Crunchbase database has 1630 registered entities based in Poland (as of 9 April 2018).

startups themselves and organisations that represent them, unlike the works published by specialised entities actively participating in startup ecosystems, such as consulting companies, startup organisations, and even startups themselves. This conclusion is supported by several facts: firstly, the small presence of representatives of the academia at large startup conferences, except for a few authorities who understand the startup world: Steve Blank (a former entrepreneur, currently an academic expert), Alexander Osterwalder (a former scientist, currently an entrepreneur), and Clayton Christensen (an academic). Secondly, one can observe low mutual citation rates between those groups of publications, that is, no references are made to hypotheses or conclusions developed by the "other" side. Perusal of both types of studies also makes the difference between the language used and the concepts applied clear, which may lead to problems with effective communication between the world of science and the world of startups. Although the startup ecosystems use a rather specific industry jargon, which should not be used in scientific studies, opening up to this language and understanding it would likely allow the scientists to better understand the issues relevant to the functioning of the companies they study. And, thus, academic studies lack appropriate suggestions for acceptable replacements (and translations) for terms typically found in the startup community jargon, for example, "pivot", "bootstrapping", "minimum viable product".

Table 2.1 presents selected non-scientific publications created by consulting companies (PwC, KPMG, Roland Berger) or organisations bringing together startup communities (Startup Fest, NASSCOM, German Startup Association), and even a consulting company that is itself a startup (Compass). These studies were selected from among many others on the basis of their methodological reliability, because many such studies are specifically accused of shortcomings in this area, consisting mainly of a totally arbitrary sample selection criteria and the size of the examined population of enterprises. This includes, for example, definitional misunderstandings (how is a startup defined) and reaching a sufficient number and variety of entities for the results to be considered credible. This is not a simple task, because official statistical data or state registers are usually useless for identifying innovative businesses, especially young and small (micro) companies. This aspect of startup research will be further discussed later.

Global consulting companies usually explore the topic of startups mostly from the point of view of their own clients. This primarily involves

Table 2.1 Selected publications of applied startup studies' results

Title of the publication	*Publication year*	*Author*	*Scope*	*Coverage*	*Description*	*Startup definition*
Global Startup Ecosystem Ranking	2015	Compass (Startup Genome)	Startup ecosystems	Worldwide	Ranking of the 20 best startup ecosystems in the world	Small and medium-sized enterprise operating online
MoneyTree Report	2016	PwC	VC transactions	Worldwide	Report on VC investments in technology companies	A company that has received VC funding and belongs to one of the 20 defined sectors
The startup economy	2013	Google and PwC	Startups and ecosystem	Australia	Identification and research of startups and recommendations for activities supporting the development of the ecosystem	Technology is central to the product or service; hyper-scalability (high revenue leverage from each additional employee), disruptive nature of product innovation, revenue under US $5 million per year
New Horizons	2015	KPMG	Startups and corporations	The Netherlands	Study of startups for their potential to collaborate with corporations	Does not define
Venture Pulse	2017	KPMG	VC transactions	Worldwide	VC Investment Market Report	Does not define
Montreal startup ecosystem report	2016	Startup Fest	Startups	Montreal	Report from a startup and startup ecosystem study	Company operating less than five years, the core of which is a scalable business model focused on innovation and digital technology

(*continued*)

Table 2.1 (continued)

Title of the publication	*Publication year*	*Author*	*Scope*	*Coverage*	*Description*	*Startup definition*
Think Act. Lessons from the Startup Nation	2016	Roland Berger	Startups and ecosystem	Israel	Best practices and data on the startup ecosystem in Israel	Does not define
Tech Startups in India	2015	NASSCOM	Startups and ecosystem	India	Report from a startup and startup ecosystem study	A business founded since 2010, owns created or acquired IP rights or creates digital trading platforms itself
European Startup Monitor	2015	German Startup Association	Startups and ecosystems	Europe	Report from a startup and startup ecosystem study	A business under ten years old; using high technologies and/or innovative business models; reports or has the potential for a significant increase in employment and/or sales
A portrait of innovative startups across countries	2018	OECD	Startups	Worldwide	Characteristics of startups from the Crunchbase database, co-financed by VC funds	Entities listed in the Crunchbase database
Polish Startups	2017	Startup Poland	Startups	Poland	Characteristics of Polish startups	An entity that works on a project in which a key element of the business model is related to broadly understood information processing technologies

Source: Own material

research on market and transactions carried out by VC funds investing in technology projects (KPMG and PwC) and, secondarily, researching startups as potential partners for corporations seeking new sources of innovation (KPMG). While perusing these reports, it is worth noticing that in nearly every case, the startups are studied together with the so-called ecosystem that surrounds them or which they create themselves. This applies to the Montreal and Berlin studies, and also to countrywide research: the Netherlands, India, and of course Israel, whose startup ecosystem is considered to be the model for those who seek ways to invigorate their own. In the case of Montreal, the research was carried out in collaboration with the municipal authorities, interested in transforming Montreal into an active startup development centre for Canada and for the whole of North America.

The following sections present selected publications in more detail.

Global Startup Ecosystem 2015 Ranking

The "Global Startup Ecosystem" ranking is created by Compass.[2] Compass itself is a startup that creates and sells automatically generated market data to enterprises. The ranking lists, as the name indicates, startup ecosystems, and not individual startups. Free to access, the ranking is created every three years, and the 2015 edition was based on 11,000 questionnaires completed by startups and investors, and 200 interviews with entrepreneurs and local experts.[3] The report ranks startup ecosystems according to five main criteria:

- ecosystem performance (30%)—calculated as the sum of the valuations of startups sold or co-financed by VC funds (80% of the score) and the number of startups in the ecosystem (20% of the score),

[2] It should be mentioned that an important source of knowledge and inspiration for the ranking is the Startup Genome project, a non-profit initiative, also a startup, which with the support of the Kauffman Foundation prepared the first information (in the form of maps) about startup ecosystems. The aim of their work was to support the sharing of knowledge serving local leaders wishing to build and develop regional startup communities. After the subsidy was stopped by the Foundation, the Startup Genome project was taken over by Compass, bringing its experience to the development of a new ranking under the Compass brand.

[3] The ranking does not include China, Taiwan, Japan, and South Korea.

Table 2.2 The results of the Global Startup Ecosystem 2015 ranking

Ecosystem	*Position*	*Change 2016/2015*	*Criteria*					*Growth index*
			Perfor-mance	*Funding*	*Market reach*	*Talent*	*Experience*	
Silicon Valley	1	Unchanged	1	1	4	1	1	2.1
New York	2	+3	2	2	1	9	4	1.8
Los Angeles	3	Unchanged	4	4	2	10	5	1.8
Boston	4	+2	3	3	7	12	7	2.7
Tel Aviv	5	−3	6	5	13	3	6	2.9
London	6	+1	5	10	3	7	13	3.3
Chicago	7	+3	8	12	5	11	14	2.8
Seattle	8	−4	12	11	12	4	3	2.1
Berlin	9	+6	7	8	19	8	8	10.0
Singapore	10	+7	11	9	9	20	9	1.9

Source: Global Startup Ecosystem, 2016

- ecosystem funding (25%)—calculated according to the total value of VC investment (80%) and the length of time needed to close a typical investment deal (20%),
- market reach (20%)—60% of this score consists of the valuation of the local market, and 40%, of the region's share in the global market,
- talent in the ecosystem (15%)—the rating of the talent consists of a quality score (80%) and, at 10% each, availability and price,[4]
- startup experience (10%)—the experience score of the ecosystem has four components with equal weights: the number of mentors who have shares in startups, the ratio of experienced startup staff among employees of startups, the percentage of startups which have among their founders a person with experience of a hyper-scalable startup, and the percentage of startups that offer their employees stock options.

The top ten ecosystems in the ranking are presented in Table 2.2. The main conclusions from the ranking are as follows:

1. The interconnectedness of startup ecosystems is growing. This is manifested in two ways: firstly, the so-called mixed investments, that is, an average of 40% of investments in startups involves at least one investor from another ecosystem; secondly, the internationalisation of founding teams: the proportion of foreigners among employees is on average 30% in the 20 largest ecosystems, and in the Silicon Valley as high as 45%.
2. When it comes to the value of transactions in the startup market, the asymmetry between the American market and the rest of the world is striking: the first five ecosystems account for 80% of the total global transaction value, and the first four ecosystems in the top five are located in the United States: the Silicon Valley, New York, Los Angeles, and Boston; Tel Aviv is in the fifth place. The average transaction value in the United States is 80% higher than in Europe. Nevertheless, the mighty American ecosystems are currently grow-

[4] The quality of the talent is calculated as the sum of the employee's experience in the startup (66%) and their skills calculated on the basis of the Top Coder country ranking (33%).

ing at a slower pace (on average by 50% annually in 2012–2014) than the much smaller European ones, growing on average by 400%, though from a significantly lower base. The average growth rate for the entire 20 is 80%. The differences in this rate are very high: in the Silicon Valley (the result most strongly influencing the total results due to its size) the growth rate in the period covered by the ranking was 50%; in London, 400%; and in Berlin, there was a 20-fold increase, caused by the formidable stock exchange debut of Zalando,[5] a part of the European (originally also German) investment vehicle[6] Rocket Internet.

3. The value of VC funds' investments in the 20 largest ecosystems in 2013–2014 doubled. The level of development of the ecosystem is important for this type of investment—it has a positive effect on both the number and the value of investments: in the mature Silicon Valley, investments in the subsequent financing rounds are growing noticeably, while the initial stage financing, the so-called seed investment, dominates in such ecosystems as Bangalore, Sydney, and Austin.

Interestingly, the share of women among founders and main startup shareholders increased from an average of 10% to as much as 18%—in just three years. Chicago has the highest ratio of female startup founders at 30%.

MoneyTree Report

This report, by the global consulting company PricewaterhouseCoopers (PwC), focuses on transactions made by VC funds in all sectors of the economy worldwide. However, as 80% of the transactions involve the top six industries, in order of frequency: Internet, health care, mobile and telecommunications technologies, other software (non-Internet and non-mobile), hardware and computer services, and electronics manufacture, it can be assumed that the report deals mainly with the ICT market.

[5] In October 2014, the German e-commerce company Zalando made its debut on the stock exchange, raising more than €600 million.

[6] This company is not easy to describe in one word; they define themselves as a "startup factory".

The main conclusions from this report are that the investment industry declined in 2016: the transactions' value decreased globally by 16% compared to the previous year, and the decline affected United States and Asia in particular, with the decrease in the United States in the last quarter of 2016 the greatest in five years. The downward trend is also affecting the industries with the highest value of investments (Internet, mobile and telecommunications technologies) and the most important investment centres (the Silicon Valley and New York). The main reasons for this state of affairs pointed out by PwC is a noticeably lower number of company valuations at the level exceeding US $1 billion (the so-called unicorns) and few really big financing rounds. On the other hand, investment in health care technologies and in artificial intelligence technologies (so-called AI) significantly increased. In Europe, unlike in the United States, the value of transactions in the last quarter of 2016 increased by more than 20%, but it is still a considerably shallower market than the United States: half the number of transactions (498 vs. 1065) and a four-times lower transaction value (US $3 billion vs. US $12 billion) in the period under consideration. In Europe as well, the investment in health care and mobile technologies is the fastest growing. Interestingly, the share of corporations in startup funding is clearly growing in Europe, which is a good reflection of the differences in trends in the startup financing structure between Europe and America (where investment funds, mainly VCs, still dominate).

The PwC Report: "The Startup Economy"

An interesting example of regional startup research is "The Startup Economy" report which focuses on the Australian ecosystem. The author—again PwC—defines the startup ecosystem as a "synergic collection (community) of startups and collaborating organisations". The Australian ecosystem study adopted a definition of a startup, according to which a startup is a company with the following characteristics: advanced technology is central to its product or service; hyper-scalable (high revenue leverage from each additional employee); "disruptive" product innovation; revenues under US $5 million a year. It must be admitted that this is a narrow and a rather demanding definition. The number of startups in Australia was estimated at only 1500, which suggests a conservative and cautious approach. The report focuses on what needs to be done in order to encourage the development of startups.

Two main solutions are suggested: in the first place, local communities should be encouraged to attract new entrepreneurs originating in the existing workforce, for example, through heavy promotion of "success stories", that is, the stories of enterprising people with a happy ending. Secondly, access to startup funding through the development of the VC market is required, as well as promoting purchasing of services from startups by large corporations and the government. In the long run, key elements stimulating the startup ecosystem include properly shaped education and improvements in the regulatory environment. It is worth emphasising that all these suggestions are very reasonable on the universal and not just Australian scale.

European Startup Monitor

This is an extensive project created by the German startup community German Startup Association, a well-developed research project covering broadly understood Europe, from Iceland to Turkey and Israel, from Portugal to Russia (its European part).[7] In addition to the general study, a detailed study is also carried out, covering 13 countries in which data are collected from a sufficient number of entities to allow general conclusions.[8] Poland is among the 13. The report is developed on the basis of a survey questionnaire completed by 2300 startups; unfortunately, the report does not contain more detailed information about the structure of this sample. According to German Startup Association, a startup is a company younger than ten years, using advanced technologies or innovative business models, and which reports (or has the potential for[9]) strong growth in employment or sales.

London, Berlin, Paris, and Tel Aviv were considered to be the largest European startup centres[10] in this report. The report has five chapters presenting data and describing the study:

- basic information about startups (location, age, development stage),
- founders and teams,

[7] The only European countries that are not covered by this study are Kosovo and Moldova.

[8] Unfortunately, there is no information as to how many exactly it means in each of these countries.

[9] This is rather difficult to determine without clear criteria.

[10] The European characters of Tel Aviv in terms of geography are quite debatable.

- startup products, customers, and markets,
- employment in startups,
- startup funding.

The sixth, additional chapter offers a commentary on the presented data and discusses the current situation, defines the challenges, and comments on the expectations of startups towards the authorities. The main attributes of European startups, according to the data from the European Startup Monitor, are:

- startups create jobs: they employ, on average, 13 people (including the founders) after 2.5 years of activity and plan rapid further growth of workforce;
- belong to the so-called digital economy industries;
- implement innovation, according to 2/3 of them—at least on the European scale;
- the founders are mostly people between 25 and 35 years old, including 15% women;
- half of the startups are engaged in exports,
- the proportion of foreigners is 12% in founding teams and 30% among the employees.

Montreal Startup Ecosystem Report

Finally, it is worth discussing the Montreal Startup Ecosystem Report. The report, which was developed as a collaboration of the local startup community and municipal authorities, aimed to, as in the case of the Australian report, propose policy tools for stimulating and encouraging the local startup ecosystem. The development of talent supplying the ecosystem and the promotion of broadly understood diversity, which stimulates innovation, are listed as the most important goals. The report also recommends pro-entrepreneurial changes in the education system, greater state participation in funding research, pro-immigration laws, promotion of attitudes accepting of uncertainty, risk, and failure, as well as minor administrative and regulatory corrections.

Startup Research Worldwide: A Summary

Studies of startups in the digital industry usually cover a similar range of research topics and research objectives. The research topics include business models and customer structure, funding sources, characteristics of founding teams, size and dynamics of employment, innovation, and propensity towards exports. Most unscientific publications also include an extensive analysis of the environment (so-called startup ecosystem), including frequent conclusions from in-depth interviews with major local startup scene players as well as development policy recommendations. The studies discussed above refer to the startup ecosystem as the environment in which startups operate and recognise its quality as a key factor for the development of startups themselves.

Research on startups and startup ecosystems is still fragmented and does not apply a unified methodology or, what is the most important, a consistent definition of the research subject—a startup. With these methodological differences, most of the studies are simply incomparable. The common denominator for most startup studies consists of two issues: the first is the imperative to estimate the importance of startups in the economy, in other words an attempt to prove that it is large and that it's growing rapidly. The second question is whether startups create jobs—if so, to what extent and if not, why not. Answers to either of these questions are not easy to find in the discussed publications. As for the first issue, there is not enough data to estimate this contribution, perhaps apart from the largest and most developed mature ecosystems, such as the Silicon Valley or Israel. As for the jobs issue, different studies provide opposite answers, but the examples of mature startups characterised by hyper-scalability suggest a low rate of job creation.

Based on the studies listed in Sect. 2.1, it is possible to propose a comparison of basic features exhibited by the entities in the three main categories of enterprises described as "startups" (Table 2.3).

In addition to the separate category of beginner companies, the comparison of the characteristics of technology enterprises (NTBFs) and digital startups gives an idea of the main differences between these two categories. The most important ones include the nature of implemented innovations (products in NTBFs vs. process-related or organisational in digital startups), the level of initial expenditures (much higher in NTBFs), the speed of entering the market (in favour of digital startups), NTBFs' dependence on access to specialised infrastructure and financing at an early

Table 2.3 Comparison of three categories of startups

Features			**Startup**: a beginner company	**Startup**: commercialisation of science (NTBF)	**Startup**: digital industry
Innovation	Overall		+	+++	+++
	including innovation:	product (R & D expenditure, patents, etc.)	+	+++	++
		process or organisation	+	++	+++
High initial expenditure			++	+++	+
Great development ambitions			+	+++	+++
Strong leadership			+	+++	+++
Creates jobs			++	++	+
Rapid development			+	++	+++
Uncertain, changing environment			+	++	+++
Instant sale			+++	+	++
Requires external financing			+	+++	++
Requires access to specialist infrastructure			+	+++	+
Requires access to highly qualified personnel			+	+++	+++
Global target market			+	+++	+++
Creates ecosystems			+	++	+++

Source: Own study based on the literature discussed in Sect. 2.1

stage of development. Both categories are described by strong leadership, high propensity to export, massive development ambitions, and a strong dependence on access to qualified, specialised workforce. On the other hand, digital startups are much more often discussed in the context of ecosystems, which boost the success chances for these enterprises.

2.2 Own Research: "Polish Startups"

Until 2015, no research of either academic or applied nature had been carried out in Poland to examine Polish startups operating in the IT and ICT industries in the widest possible, and ideally, a comprehensive scope. Partial studies were published by such authors as Leszek Bursiak (2013, 2014), Ewa Badzińska (2014, 2015), Monika Burżacka and Elżbieta Gąsiorowska

(2015), Agata Gemzik-Salwach (2014a, b), and Jarosław Korpysa (2012). These studies were not free of the defect discussed in this publication, that is, the individual interpretation of the concept of a "startup". There were also no other studies—neither foreign nor non-academic—concerning this growing and at that time, self-organising, group of enterprises. Having determined the existence of this research gap, the author of this book decided to design, prepare, and carry out her own research project in this area.

This undertaking, which was soon named "Polish Startups", was the first comprehensive survey of startups in the Polish digital industry (ICT). From a long-term perspective, this research project aims to provide a solution to the research problem, namely, the determination of the importance of startups for the economy of Poland and the region. The research project consists of primary research of a quantitative and qualitative nature, which aims to describe Polish startups. The research should include the largest possible, and, ultimately, representative sample of startups.

The first step in the project was a pilot study, which provided an opportunity to verify the first version of the questionnaire and carry out in-depth interviews with expert respondents. This topic is elaborated on later in this chapter.

During the pilot study, the author established a close collaboration with the Startup Poland Foundation, which was created at the same time (i.e. in 2015), and since then, has associated and represented the interests of the startup community in Poland. The Foundation is a grass-roots initiative of people involved in the development of the Polish startup ecosystem, with statutory goals that include promoting startup entrepreneurship, popularising entrepreneurial attitudes, undertaking measures aimed at increasing the innovativeness of the Polish economy, as well as scientific activity serving those goals. As a result of the collaboration with the Foundation, it was decided to carry out a comprehensive analysis of the Polish startup scene, with the support of the Foundation in terms of building a database (a list) of startups in Poland and a wide-reaching campaign for the distribution of the research questionnaire. The Foundation is also the publisher of the research report, and thanks to promotional activities carried out by the Foundation, the report reaches many people and institutions nationally and abroad. The author is responsible for all methodological and substantive aspects of the "Polish Startups" study (including the final text of the reports).

The study has been run six times so far, including one pilot study, four full editions in Poland and one edition abroad. In 2016, cooperation

Table 2.4 Stages of the "Polish Startups" research project

Research stage	*Date*	*Number of questions in the questionnaire*	*Number of respondents*	*Response rate*
Pilot (Gieżyńska and Skala 2016)	May 2015	36	38	53%
First edition of the study (Kruczkowska et al. 2015)	June–September 2015	36	423	17%
Second edition of the study (Kruczkowska and Skala 2016)	July–August 2016	48	692	26%
Third edition of the study (Beauchamp et al. 2017)	June–August 2017	69	764	29%
Visegrád Group study (Beauchamp and Skala 2017)	June 2016–April 2017	Basic version: 33	980	No data
Fourth edition of the study (Beauchamp et al. 2018)	June–July 2018	89	1101	41%

Source: Own material

began with equivalent to Startup Poland institutions in the Czech Republic, Slovakia, and Hungary, which led to a field study and a publication of a report on startups in the Visegrád Group states (which will be discussed later in this chapter). Table 2.4 presents the successive stages of the project.

Method

At the stage of designing the startup study, the main goals were the development of the questionnaire and the correct selection of respondents. These two key factors were to ensure the highest possible number of credible and complete answers to the research questions posed.

The Questionnaire

The questionnaire was developed on the basis of the knowledge acquired from the (discussed earlier) research carried out abroad, and the author's own knowledge. The latter was a result of many years of direct and open participatory observation of the startup community in Poland: the author of the study has been an active member of the Polish startup community since 2010, including her role as a member of the Policy Board of the Startup Poland Foundation, as well as a startup mentor and educator, an observer of trends in this market, an organiser and participant in many events that take place in the startup community.[11] The structure, form, and content of the survey were particularly important because it was assumed that the success of the study depends to a large extent on the proper formulation of the questions (cf. Januszkiewicz 2016). Startups, as already mentioned, are more and more often a subject of research and surveys, run by consulting companies or scientists who collect data for their studies. Familiarity with the startup culture meant that the author realised that using language understandable for the founders of startups and raising problems that the entrepreneurs themselves consider important was crucial for collecting valuable data. The Startup Poland Foundation shared this belief, which led to the Foundation becoming a partner in the research project. The goal of the pilot study was to test the first version of the questionnaire. After the pilot, the questionnaire was subject to evaluation by the so-called competent judges, in this case, experts specialising in startups. Some of the experts' suggestions were incorporated into the questionnaire. The questionnaire used in the first edition of the study in 2015 contained 36 questions. Most of them were multiple choice and included a space for additional, open-ended comments. This was a purposeful choice and intended to generate improvements in the subsequent versions of the questionnaire, which was actually done.

Sample Selection

Correct sample selection was one of the main challenges facing the project. Previous research in the Warsaw high-tech enterprise sector had shown that the process of identifying entities qualifying for research in innovative and high-technology sectors was complicated, because one could not rely on the statistical data available in the National Business Registry Number (REGON register) (cf. Skala 2014). Prior to the pilot study, an initial study was carried out to identify the codes from the Polish Classification of Activities (PKD) reported by the startups when registering in the National Court Register (KRS). If it turned

[11] For example, Aula Polska, ReaktorX, InnoShare, Startup Weekend, Startup Weekend Next, and others.

out that startups register themselves consistently using specific PKD numbers, then these numbers would be a reliable and convenient way to identify digital economy startups. A total of 138 registered startups were examined, whose names were taken from publicly accessible databases: the list of winners of startup competitions (Aulery and Startup Weekend) and a list of startups voluntarily registered in the Startup Poland Foundation database (as of April 2015). This initial analysis resulted in the following findings:

- More than 40% of the examined companies (82) did not provide a code for the dominant activity in the KRS register.
- Among startups which did provide an activity code (56 companies), activity in the following PKD groups was reported by 38 startups (68% of this group)—PKD 62: "Computer programming activities, computer consultancy activities and related activities" and PKD 63: "Information-related services",
- Thus, in 100 out of the 138 examined startups (almost ¾ of the population) the PKD code was undefined, not available, or not associated with PKD numbers 62 or 63.
- It was decided that in this situation, the PKD code was not a sufficient or reliable criterion for identifying digital startups.

To sum up, just over half of the examined entities declared that they were doing business within PKD numbers 62 or 63, but the other half either did not attach any importance to it (did not declare any kind of activity in the National Court Register) or did not think that the number correctly reflected the nature of their business. This could result in serious mistakes in the analysis carried out on the basis of sectoral affiliation (i.e. according to PKD). The same problem was encountered when carrying out research in the high-tech sector, where the PKD number in half of the cases did not reflect the actual profile of the company's business (Rostek and Skala 2014).

A startup was defined as an entity that works on a project in which a key element of the business model is related to broadly understood information processing technologies. Projects not yet formally registered were also considered to be startups if they met the criteria mentioned earlier. A Polish startup was defined as one that was (or would be) registered in Poland or one with at least one co-founder who was a citizen of Poland. In the latter case, a startup had to meet an additional condition, and at least partially carry out their activities in Poland (e.g. produce software). A branch of a company whose head office was located abroad was not considered to be a Polish startup.

The problem of reaching correct respondents at the pilot stage was resolved in the following way: invitations to fill out the questionnaires were sent only to those enterprises which had taken part in startup competitions or had among their founders a person who had founded a company in this industry before. For the purpose of further research, a database of startups was created using a "bottom-up" method, without resorting to central registers. The names of the entities were obtained from the following sources: VC funds, accelerators, business incubators, technology parks, training companies, organisers of startup competitions, Polish Agency for Enterprise Development (PARP) and The National Centre for Research and Development in Poland (NCBR) grant lists, lists from industry media websites, as well as from private rankings and databases of "startup activists". It was the first such extensive campaign aiming to estimate the number of startups in Poland. Each lead obtained in this way was verified by checking it in the KRS database and on the company's own website, at the same time obtaining contact details in the form of an e-mail address and telephone numbers. An e-mail was sent twice to each verified startup from the Startup Poland database, containing a request to complete the questionnaire, and one or two telephone follow-ups were also made. Representatives of the startups could also find out about the survey from the media and from social networking sites (e.g. Facebook and Twitter).

A two-tier selection process was applied to the sample.

- the first tier utilised the carefully selected channels discussed above in order to reach startups with an invitation to participate in the survey;
- the second tier of selection took place in the introduction to the questionnaire, where the respondent had to answer the question determining whether the project he or she would talk about was a startup as defined in the study design; the criteria for answering "yes" or "no" were clearly explained in the question; a negative answer terminated the survey.

In 80–85% of cases, the questionnaire was completed, as recommended, by persons who were founders (or co-founders) and/or Chief Executive Officers (CEOs) of the companies. Other respondents were most often members of the firm's Management Board, and occasionally product managers, sales managers or Board of Directors' assistants.

A variety of data analysis methods was used in the project. The quantitative data was analysed using the tools available as part of the webankieta.pl website, which was used to collect the responses, as well as mathematical and statistical methods using a spreadsheet or SPSS Statistics. Responses to the open-ended questions were coded according to keywords and analysed using frequency distributions for individual statements.

Pilot Study

The pilot study was performed in May 2015. Seventy-two requests to complete the survey were sent and 38 responses were received, which meant a high (above 50%) response rate. Such a response rate was achieved by sending the requests to complete the questionnaire exclusively to contacts from the author's network of personal and professional acquaintances. It was requested that the survey should be completed by the startup's leader. Only in one case the questionnaire was completed by the head of marketing; in all other cases the respondents were as requested. All answers, except for the name of the startup and the respondent's role, were non-compulsory. Despite that, only in few cases questions were left unanswered.

The survey was divided into three parts. The first aimed to develop a general characteristic of the examined enterprises and was more extensive (15 questions). The second covered issues related to the topic of convergence of startups with the characteristics of the high-tech sector (nine questions). The first two parts consisted of closed or predefined questions, but in each appropriate case the respondent was given the opportunity to add their own answer or comment. Open questions were used for the name of the startup, the website address, a one-sentence description of the nature of the business, and so on. The third and last part of the survey was dedicated to innovation and how it was created in startups. Four open questions were included to investigate the essence of the innovation created by the startup, the nature of R&D in the startup, and how it was carried out. The results from the pilot study were published and presented at the "Digital Ecosystems" scientific conference organised by the Digital Economy Laboratory of the University of Warsaw (DELab) in June 2015 (Gieżyńska and Skala 2016).

Results of the 2015–2018 Research[12]

The large-scale study proper was made possible by the involvement of the[13] newly created Startup Poland Foundation as a project partner. The Foundation committed to the participation in building a startup database, to promoting the study among startups using its contacts and communication channels, and to funding the work on the report and its publication and distribution. Numerous regional and local startup communities collaborating with the Foundation, as well as industry media, also became involved in the study. As a result, during the four years of the project, approximately 2,000 entities were surveyed (some of the startups participated in the study every year). Such a wide reach is the greatest achievement of this research project, unprecedented in research on startups in Poland.[14]

The study covered six main areas:

- basic data of the startups: location, period of operation, legal form, and stage of development;
- business models: customer categories, sales models, and main types of products and services;
- resources: sources of capital, revenues, and non-financial resources;
- exports;
- innovation: patents and collaboration with the academia;
- human resources: characteristics of partners and employees.

The study has been subject to analysis and improvement throughout the project's entire lifetime. This leads, on the one hand, to the collection of increasingly more precise data, but, on the other hand, it means that some results are not comparable. After the first edition of the study between March and April 2016, a new version of the questionnaire was developed, based on the author's own knowledge and the experience from the previous edition of the study. In the first half of May 2016, the questionnaires were developed for the section of the study repeated in the

[12] The results of the 2018 survey have not yet been elaborated.

[13] The Foundation was registered in April 2015.

[14] For example, the Deloitte report from 2016 "Diagnosis of startups ecosystem in Poland" was based on the study of about 70 companies that meet certain conditions for being called digital startups.

Visegrád Group states. The final version of the Polish questionnaire contained 48 questions, most of which were single or multiple choice. The survey contained routing filters which meant that some questions were only asked of the respondents who gave specific answers in preceding questions. Apart from five questions, answers to all other questions were voluntary (i.e. it was possible to skip questions without terminating the survey).

The current (end of 2018) state of knowledge about startups, on the basis of all the editions of the study so far, is as follows (based on: Beauchamp et al. 2018):

- more startups take part in the study every year: the reach of the study increases by approximately 20% per annum;
- Warsaw is the main startup centre (a startup hub) in Poland, but four other cities are also significant: Wrocław, Kraków, Poznań, and Trójmiasto;
- the startup generation is growing up: 53% of the survey respondents are 30-somethings, the share of older people is growing, and the share of 20-somethings is decreasing (29%);
- 88% of the startup founders have university degrees, including 6% with a doctoral degree or higher;
- the startup founders have gained their professional experience mainly in their own or family businesses, in corporations, or while developing a previous startup;
- founders of every fifth startup include at least one scientist, every third startup has a woman among its founders, one in eight a foreigner;
- 84% of the startups operate in a business-to-business model (so-called B2B), that is, they sell technologies and services to other companies, and those customer companies are getting larger and larger;
- most startups create products in the areas of Big Data, business analytics, Internet of Things, and tools for developers;
- every fourth startup manufactures electronic equipment, that is, hardware;
- Polish startups most often generate regular revenues from design and fashion, tools for developers, and marketing technologies;
- startups operating in natural sciences, health care, and biotechnology sectors obtain regular revenues least frequently;
- more than 40% of the startups have regular income, of which 41% generate average monthly revenues above PLN 100,000 (approxi-

mately €23,000) and 20% of them grow at least 50% per month (in terms of revenue level);

- the percentage of startups that develop with the help of external capital is falling; 60% of startups are funded from their own equity and revenues only;
- among those that have obtained external financing, 40% have obtained more than PLN 1 million (approximately €230,000);
- every fifth startup participates in public procurement;
- three-quarters of the startups are commercial law companies (limited liability or joint stock companies);
- the most valued sources of knowledge are individual mentoring and meetings of startup communities and the least valued are classes and incubators at universities;
- the most desirable resource, critical for the development of startups, is access to a qualified workforce;
- almost half of the surveyed Polish startups export their products and services, mainly to the European Union (EU) (59%) and the United States (23%);
- the exporters grow faster, earn more, and find it easier to attract investors; among the exporters as many as 60% generate regular revenues and more than half belong to the group with the highest revenues;
- 30% of the surveyed startups do not employ anybody, half are micro-enterprises, and 20% employ more than ten people;
- 28% of the startups employ staff from abroad (the trend is upwards), primarily from the Ukraine (46%), the United States, and the United Kingdom;
- nearly half of the surveyed startups report collaboration with the academia, and 19% patent their solutions, of which over half do it abroad (both indicators are increasing).
- the most popular sources of knowledge for the startups include industry reports, internal strategic sessions, prototype building, interviews with clients, and expert consultations;
- few startups carry out (commission) quantitative or qualitative market research; however, they often read industry reports—only one in four do not use this source of knowledge.

The most important indicators from the three editions of the study are shown in Table 2.5.

Table 2.5 Main characteristics of the study and the surveyed startups—data indicators from the "Polish Startups" study

Characteristic	*2015*	*2016*	*2017*	*2018*
Number of startups in the Startup Poland database	2432	2677	2677	2677
Total number of respondents	423	692	764	1101
Number of eligible respondents	423	539	629	806
Percentage of eligible respondents (%)				
Survey completed by the CEO/startup founder	80	85	86	85
Startup sells only in the B2B model	*57*	51	57	49
Startup sells only in the B2C model	*28*	18	18	14
Startup sells in the SaaS[a] model	39	33	39	40
Startup designs and/or manufactures hardware	*11*	20	25	24
Startup sells in e-commerce model	*22*	14	16	19
Startup creates software for mobile technologies	*24*	14	14	15
Startup uses funding from own resources only	*60*	50	62	59
Startup uses EU co-financing	23	*24*	38	40
Startup uses co-financing from VC funds (venture capital)	*18*	*22*	40	37
Startup uses BA (business angel) financing	*20*	*17*	33	26
Startup has regular revenues	No data	44	41	40
Exports	54	47	48	46
Startup is a micro-enterprise (employs 1–10 people)	64	59	49	53
Startup does not employ anyone	17	22	29	29
Founder of the startup is aged 30–40 years old	No data	53	58	53
Startup has a woman among founders	28	26	29	26
Startup has an academic (at least a PhD) among the founders	15	13	20	18
Startup patents its solutions	*35*	14	19	18
Startup cooperates with an academic/research centre	*25*	42	46	44

The answers marked in italics are not fully comparable due to the change in the wording of the question or the response options

[a]SaaS: Software as a Service

Source: Own study based on "Polish Startups" reports 2015–2018

As part of the third study edition in 2017, 11 research hypotheses were posed, the verification of which was to provide in-depth knowledge about Polish startups. The hypotheses and the results of their verification are presented in Table 2.6.

The main conclusion from the analysis so far is that the startup market is clearly maturing and becoming more professional. The share of the startups which offer solutions for business, and for larger companies in particular—a more stable and a more solvent type of a customer—is increasing. The startup founders, more mature in personal

Table 2.6 Auxiliary hypotheses and the results of their verification in the "Polish Startups" study in 2017

Auxiliary hypothesis	*Verification results*
H1: Most of the surveyed startups do not sell abroad	Positive: Nearly half of the sample (48%) export Additional data: The main causes for deciding against expansion beyond the Polish market were listed as (according to importance): The desire to "test" the product on the local market (approximately 60% of responses from startups that do not export); Insufficient financial, human, or competence resources (33% responses); Insufficient network of contacts abroad (27%); The product is not ready (15%); The nature of the product is local (10%)
H2: The majority of surveyed startups have regular revenues	Negative: 44% of the startups reported regular income Additional data: Among the regular earners, almost 60% earn up to PLN 100,000 per month, while 15% over PLN 500,000 per month
H3: There is a difference in turnover between exporting and non-exporting startups in favour of the former	Positive: Compared with the exporters, significantly fewer non-exporters report regular income: 60% and 22% respectively; In the group of exporters, half of the respondents (49%) declare an average monthly income under PLN 100,000 in the previous six months; in the group of startups that operate locally, as many as 81% of the respondents do not exceed that level of revenues; 19% of the exporters are top earners (on average above PLN 500,000 per month), while only 3% of the non-exporters report revenues at that level Thus, it can be said that, firstly, the exporters earn much more regularly and, secondly, that their average income is certainly higher than is the case for the non-exporting startups

(*continued*)

Table 2.6 (continued)

Auxiliary hypothesis	*Verification results*
H4: Surveyed startups that struggle with a shortage of employees in the market employ foreigners, especially from the Ukraine and the UK	Partially confirmed Among the surveyed startups, 42% indicate access to personnel as the most desirable resource at the current stage of their development. At the same time, 28% of the respondents employ foreigners. Analysis of the data also indicates that: There is no significant correlation between the need for access to human resources and hiring foreigners; in other words, the data do not indicate that it's specifically the startups struggling with staff shortages that seek employees abroad; Foreigners are employed mainly by startups that export, have foreign co-founders, or are incorporated abroad; The foreign employees come mainly from the Ukraine (39%), the United States (25%), and the United Kingdom (15%) A deeper analysis of the data allows for stating another thesis, namely that: Employees from the United Kingdom and especially from the United States are connected to a foreign expansion of the startups and are "experts"; Employing staff from the Ukraine is more often related to the shortage of qualified staff in Poland and those employees actually represent additional "hands on deck"
H5: Startups that took part in the survey need employees with sales skills	Positive: Firstly, as already stated in point 2., 42% of the startups lists access to workers as the most desired resource at the current stage of their development; When asked about skills sought in potential employees, the respondents most often list programmers, developers, and so on (72%), as well as salespeople (52%) and marketing specialists (40%) Thus, startups need employees with sales skills, especially ones with knowledge and experience in sales abroad

(*continued*)

Table 2.6 (continued)

Auxiliary hypothesis	*Verification results*
H6: Most startups do not patent their solutions	Positive: Generally, relatively few solutions in the digital industry are patentable. Therefore, the startups build their competitive advantage in ways other than registering industrial property rights. Patents are associated with startups that manufacture products related to the medical and electronic industries These conclusions were confirmed by the survey results: The group of startups which register patents is dominated by the companies that manufacture products in the areas of Life Science/Healthcare/Biotechnology, Internet of Things/Electronics/Robotics, and Big Data; the startups which do not register patents mostly point to the unpatentability of their solutions (63%), while every fourth "does not see the value in patents". The remaining two reasons are product not ready for applying for a patent (but there is an intention for the future, at 15%) and lack of financial resources for this purpose (9%)
H7: The surveyed startups that do not take part in public procurement as bidders do not do it because in their opinion it is too time-consuming compared to acquiring another customer	Negative: The most important reason for which the tested startups do not take part in public procurement as bidders is the nature of their product, which means that public procurement tenders do not apply to them (39% indications among startups that do not participate in tenders). The second reason mentioned by the respondents is the time-consuming nature of the process (25%). Further reasons are (in the descending number of indications) lack of information about tenders (18%), insufficient skills (18%), lack of resources (17%), lack of product readiness, fear of bureaucratic red tape, and a belief that tenders are "fixed"
H8: For the surveyed startups which are involved in public procurement, it is an important source of income	Negative: 70 startups which carried out a public procurement contract (won the tender and completed the order) were identified. It should be noted that this is not a large population For two-thirds of them (67%), the public contracts revenue made up no more than 25% of their total revenue, and for 84% of this group made no more than half of the revenue. That is, only for 16% of the startups that take part in public procurement, public contracts account for more than 50% of revenues

(*continued*)

Table 2.6 (continued)

Auxiliary hypothesis	*Verification results*
H9: The cooperation between surveyed startups and research institutions is mostly informal	Negative: The sample contained 259 startups (42% of all respondents) working with a university, an R&D centre other than a university, or individually with an academic researcher. In 55% of these cases, the startups stated that this collaboration was formalised. Every third said it was not formalised, while more than 10% stated that it was difficult to say or that it did not matter. Asked if it would be better if the collaboration was formalised, half of the respondents thought that it wasn't necessary or that they "weren't bothered". A quarter of the respondents expressed the opposite opinion
H10: Among the surveyed Polish startups which acquired external financing, the total amount of funding per startup does not exceed PLN 500,000	Negative: The average amount of external financing is higher Amounts not exceeding PLN 500,000 were reported by every third (34%) startup that uses external financing. Most startups (60%) declare financing not exceeding double of that amount, that is, below PLN 1,000,000
H11: Most startup founders have a minority share in their startup	Negative: First of all, the majority (62%) of surveyed startups do not have investors at all, so the founders own all of the shares. In contrast, among those who have external financing (38%), only in 20% the founders have a minority stake (up to 50% of the shares)

Source: Own material

and professional sense, are able to afford to support their businesses on their own, especially as they don't have to wait for the first income for as long as they used to. Getting to the stage of business scaling forces startups to seek external financing, which comes noticeably later. The investors' resources are used to, first of all, employ new specialists, an increasingly more difficult challenge for the founders. This favours the import of human resources from abroad, which in turn stimulates the positive trend towards a growing (though still low) cultural diversity and opening up to the world. Export is the most effective springboard for the development of a startup, which has been confirmed for the third time (Beauchamp et al. 2017, p. 95).

2.3 Own Research: Startups in the Visegrád Group Countries[15]

The developments in research on Polish startups and the expansion of the activity and collaborative relationships of the Startup Poland Foundation in the Visegrád region created the opportunity to carry out an equivalent study in other countries: the Czech Republic, Slovakia, and Hungary. The author was again responsible for the methodological and substantive aspects of the project, while the organisation and publication were handled by the Foundation. Before the study proper, a brief analysis of the conditions for innovative business was carried out, which was to help in understanding the functioning of startups in this region. The analysis included the traditional indicators describing the condition of the economy in these countries, their development potential and digital habits of the residents, as well as qualitative indicators that illustrated the level of activity and engagement of local startup communities in the countries covered by the study.

The analysis used primary data from Eurostat and two reputable secondary sources in the form of rankings: *Doing Business* (World Bank 2017), which assesses the general business environment and the *Global Innovation Index* (*GII*), which lists factors relevant to innovative business. Data on local entrepreneurial ecosystems was obtained directly from the participant institutions and organisations and locally from the partners of the Startup Poland Foundation in the Visegrád countries: *Aspen Institute Central Europe* (in the Czech Republic), *Hungarian Startups* and *Global Traction* (in Hungary), *The Slovak Alliance for the Innovative Economy: SAPIE.sk* (in Slovakia).

It is worth presenting the most important conclusions from this analysis.

Conditions for Startups: Macroeconomic Data[16]

The most important macroeconomic data which determine the functioning of startups in the Visegrád countries are presented in Table 2.7.

[15] Based on the working material for Beauchamp and Skala (2017).

[16] Based on Eurostat data from 2016.

Table 2.7 Conditions for the functioning of startups in the Visegrád countries (2016)—macroeconomic data

Domain	*Determinants*
Economy	In terms of the pace of economic development (calculated in terms of real GDP growth), Poland and Slovakia grew relatively fastest in the Visegrád region (about 3% per year), while the Czech Republic and Hungary developed at the level of the EU average (2% and 1.6%, respectively)
	The level of investments made by enterprises does not differ from the EU average (approximately 20–25% of GDP), and in the Czech Republic it reaches almost 25%. The highest individual consumption is reported in Poland (59% of GDP), and the lowest in the Czech Republic (47%); nevertheless, it is around the EU average of 56%
	As far as the average level of wealth (calculated as GDP per capita in relation to the EU average) is concerned, the best situation is in the Czech Republic (the average Czech lives at 87% of the average EU citizen), and then in Slovakia (77%). Poland and Hungary reach a level slightly below 70% of the EU average
	Unemployment is a significant problem in Slovakia (8.4%), but at the same time in this country, the productivity of labour is the highest among the Visegrád countries, none of which achieves an EU average in this respect. In all four countries, young graduates of schools or universities find jobs without much difficulty. The employment rate, or occupational activity of the residents, is at the EU level (around 70%), while in the Czech Republic it is noticeably higher (77%)
	All countries have a positive trade balance, that is, the value of their exports exceeds the value of imports
Population	Over 63 million people live in the Visegrád countries, which amounts to every 12th EU resident. Poles constitute 60% of the population of the region (just under 38 million), Czechs and Hungarians make up 16% each (10 million each), and 8% are Slovaks (5.5 million)
	While three out of four Czechs live in a city, only half of Slovaks do. In Hungary, 71% of the population live in cities, and in Poland, 61%
	The enrolment rate at the university level is the highest in Poland: almost half of Poles aged 30–34 years old are university graduates. In other countries, it is approximately a third of this age group

(*continued*)

Table 2.7 (continued)

Domain	*Determinants*
Digitisation	Access to broadband Internet in the Visegrád countries does not differ from the EU average. The Internet access for households is high in all those countries (76–80%), although at a slightly lower level than the EU average (83%). With regard to enterprises, it is similar, and high, at over 90% in the entire region
	Approximately 80% of residents use the Internet regularly; only in Poland this figure is lower at about 70%. Poland and Hungary also have the highest proportion of people who do not use the Internet at all (one in five people). Poland is also the worst in terms of the use of mobile technologies, which are used only by a third of Poles, while in other countries 50–60% of the residents use mobile technologies
	35–40% of Poles and Hungarians use digital banking, while in the Czech Republic and Slovakia more than half of the residents do. Similar figures describe the use of online resources such as films, images, games, and so on, with Poles (28%) again falling behind the Czechs and Slovaks (45%), as well as Hungarians (35%). Looking for work online is rare in the Czech Republic and Slovakia (only 5% people search for jobs in this way), while 10% of Poles and 17% of Hungarians use this form of job seeking
	Poles and Hungarians are less active as e-commerce customers (about 40% vs. 47% in the Czech Republic and Slovakia and 55% in the EU on average). For this reason the share of enterprises' revenues from online trading is on average 15% in Poland and Hungary, and 30% in the Czech Republic and Slovakia. Interestingly, this is twice as much as the EU average. The same pattern applies to the percentage of enterprises accepting online orders: 27% in the Czech Republic and Slovakia, and 12% in Poland and Hungary
	Countries with smaller populations generally report better results in terms of digitisation than those with larger populations, which is why the Czech Republic and Slovakia are significantly better in this respect than Hungary, and especially Poland

(*continued*)

Table 2.7 (continued)

Domain	*Determinants*
Innovation	In the V4 Group, Czechs spend the highest proportion of their GDP on R&D (just under 2% of the GDP), while Poles spend the least (1%). The EU average is over 2% It is interesting to divide this expenditure between the public and private sectors: in Hungary, where the contribution from government funds is extremely low (only 0.18%), private enterprises allocated more than five times as much to R&D. In the Czech Republic, business allocates more than three times than the public sector, which is much more generous there than in Hungary (0.4% of GDP). In Slovakia, public and private expenditure balance exactly (0.33% GDP each), while in Poland the private sector spends twice as much on R&D as the amount of government spending, which reaches 0.25% of the GDP Apart from the Czech Republic (the indicator there is above the EU average), the remaining countries are weak in terms of the proportion of R&D staff in the workforce—and this indicator says a lot about the realistic possibilities for creating innovative solutions in the economy. In Hungary, this rate reaches two-thirds of the EU level; in Poland, three-fifths; and in Slovakia, only half. This result translates into the number of patent applications, which in the discussed countries is dramatically lower than the EU average, where there are 112 applications per 1 million inhabitants. In the Czech Republic it is 26, in Hungary 23, in Poland 16, and in Slovakia only 9

Source: Own material based on: Eurostat and (Beauchamp and Skala 2017)

Conditions for Startups: Innovation and Business

The *Doing Business* ranking, developed by the World Bank, is a recognised source of information on the "ease" of setting up and running a business in almost all countries in the world (specifically, it covers 189 countries.) The report identifies the number, duration, and cost of procedures that entrepreneurs must carry out to perform 11 identified tasks (steps) related to hypothetical business operations: from founding a company, to hiring workers, obtaining a loan and a building permit, to closing the business. This ranking enjoys the reputation of a credible and practical source of information.

In the 14th (2017) edition of the ranking (data for 2016), the highest (best) position was achieved by Poland (24th), followed by the Czech Republic (27th), Slovakia (33rd), and Hungary (41st). Breaking the general score into 11 business-related domains shows similarities, but also significant differences, between the surveyed countries. The optimal situation occurs when the curve for a given country runs "low" and is as flat as possible. Since 2010, the Czech Republic and Poland have improved their position in this ranking the fastest.

The position of a given country in the GII ranking is the average of the results of two groups of indicators: "input" and "output". The former includes indicators that describe the conditions for undertaking innovation: stability of law and institutions, development of human capital and the R&D sphere, saturation with infrastructure, market, and business sophistication. The "output" indicators provide an overview of the effects of the undertaken activities: creation and expansion of knowledge and technology-based economy and creative outputs. The Czech Republic in 2015 was in the prestigious Top 25; unfortunately it lost this place and a year later slipped by two places. Poland scores the worst among the four, but it has made the most progress in the analysed period and has moved up to the top 40. It does not change the fact that the ranking is based on strong methodological foundations, and is developed by the best research centres, and Poland's position is simply weak, while the progress is insufficient to recognise Poland as an innovative country on the basis of GII.

The GII ranking indicates the strongest and the weakest innovation factors for each of the surveyed countries. The analysis of those factors for the Visegrád countries does not lead to optimistic conclusions. The strengths of the V4 region countries usually do not relate to important indicators, which appear more often in the context of the weaknesses of the discussed countries. Visegrád countries have a strong position in the domain of production and export of goods and services saturated with technology, which, however, results more from the factories located in the area (especially in the Czech Republic and Hungary), and not necessarily from innovation in the sense of designing products and deriving benefits from, for example, intellectual property. The domain of *Creative Outputs* and *Knowledge & Technology Outputs* also scores well.

The weaknesses include education-related indicators, including an insufficient number of STEM graduates[17]—despite the universally recognised high quality of STEM education in the countries of the region, their share in the total number of students is relatively low. The worst rated innovation domain in the Visegrád countries is *Market and Business*

[17] STEM—Science, Technology, Engineering, and Mathematics.

Sophistication, especially the low indicators for foreign and mixed investments and strategic alliances.

It can also be said that a more detailed analysis of the capital market indicators clearly indicates its immaturity and low accumulation of capital as a serious barrier to the development of innovative business in the entire region, while insufficient openness to external capital, or low interest in investing in this region from foreign capital does not compensate for local shortcomings. Thus, the market of VCs and other forms of entities investing in innovative ventures, as well as the number of transactions and their internationalisation, remain at a very low level in this region.

Comparative Analysis of Startups in the Visegrád Countries[18]

Approximately 860 startups participated in the Visegrád Startup Survey carried out by Startup Poland. The data collected are a good starting point for more detailed and more methodologically sound research projects in the future.

The study confirms that a typical founder of a startup is an experienced professional around 30 years old. Especially in Poland and the Czech Republic, this age group dominates among the startup founders. Over two-thirds of them have a bachelor's or higher degree, and half (in the Czech Republic) or one-third (in Slovakia) founded another startup in the past. Slovakia has the highest percentage of women among the respondents, at approximately 30%, while Hungary, with just 11% women, is the most "male-dominated" startup scene in the surveyed group of countries. The country capitals are also the biggest startup centres with a high concentration of human and capital resources: Prague, Budapest, and Bratislava attract the majority of local startups. The second most active startup city in the Czech Republic is Brno, while in Poland, the largest of the four countries, startup communities are very active in four other metropolitan areas: Kraków, Wrocław, Poznań, and Trójmiasto. Apart from a limited liability company, which is the most popular legal form for the surveyed startups (70% overall), many companies register their businesses as joint stock companies (most common in Slovakia at 17% and in Hungary at 15%) or as sole proprietorships (18% respondents in Poland).

[18] Chapter section based on Beauchamp and Skala (2017).

Poland and the Czech Republic reported more startups at the stage of full business maturity than Hungary or Slovakia. One-third of the startups surveyed in Poland and the Czech Republic, and one-fifth in Hungary and Slovakia, do not employ any staff at all. More than half of all surveyed startups are micro-enterprises employing up to ten people. In Poland and the Czech Republic, micro-enterprises dominate the surveyed population even more and account for, respectively, 75% and 66% of the surveyed startups.

The startups were asked to describe their customer structure. The surveyed startups focus on many customer segments, for example, they develop multilateral business models. Despite this, business remains the main customer of startups, in particular large companies, including corporations (40–50% of startups choose this type of customer). Interestingly, the survey revealed that public institutions are an important category of customers (so-called Business-to-Government—B2G), especially for startups in the Czech Republic and Slovakia, less frequently in Poland, and almost never in Hungary.

The data from Slovakia, the Czech Republic, and Poland confirm that approximately 70–80% of local startups reinvest their income. Some raise external financing: only 6.5% of Czech startups, 15% in Slovakia, 22% in Poland, and 25% in Hungary use local (national) VC funds. In each of the surveyed countries, about 15% of the startups use financing from BAs. While the level of public funding is the lowest among Czech startups (8%), this share is relatively higher for Polish ventures (24%). Very few startups in Hungary (2%), in the Czech Republic (3%), and in Slovakia (9%) use academic grants. As many as 11% of startup projects in Slovakia are financed by crowdfunding—the highest percentage in the region.

One in three startups in the Czech Republic and Slovakia and every fourth in Poland and Hungary collaborate with a university. At the same time, approximately 10–15% of surveyed startups consult the development of their products with an R&D institution (academic or commercial). Interestingly, most of these consultations, in particular with the academic world, are clearly informal and are not reported in university administration registers. Every fourth startup in Slovakia and one in three in the Czech Republic have a patent for their invention or a registered trademark.

The study has confirmed the general principle that countries with a lower domestic demand are more likely to export their goods and services. Startups from the Czech Republic and Slovakia export much more frequently (75–80% of the respondents) than their counterparts from Hungary or Poland (65% and nearly 50% respectively). What's most interesting, exporters in each country are dominated by two distinctive groups: one that is dominated by startups exporting only a small proportion of their products or services (less than 30% of sales) and another that sees the export market as the main source of revenue (over 80% of sales). Not many startups consider Asia to be the best export market (only 3% in Poland and Hungary). The main export directions are the markets of the EU and the United States.

A summary analysis of strengths and weaknesses of each of the surveyed countries is presented in Table 2.8.

It is worth monitoring and supporting the development of startups in the digital industry in Poland and in the world on the basis of reliable data rather than "common wisdom". This is a real challenge, given the lack of clarity as to the basic definitions of the research subject and the research methodology. The research carried out in cooperation with the Startup Poland Foundation since 2015 provides knowledge which builds a real picture of this market at the national as well as regional level.

2.4 The Main Characteristics Differentiating Startups

Further analysis of the results of the "Polish Startups" research aimed to identify the main characteristics that describe and differentiate startups. To this end, the data obtained in the first and second edition of the study were subjected to in-depth segmentation analysis using three methods: clustering, self-organising Kohonen networks, and cluster analysis (Rostek and Skala 2017). The analysis took place in two stages—first on the basis of data from the first edition (2015), and then on the basis of the combined data from the first and the second edition (2015 and 2016). In the first round, the segmentation included 131 nominal variables and 416 entities, and the segmentation was carried out in regard of the differentiating factors, but without indicating the superordinate variable (in other words target variable) for the grouping. The results defined the most important subgroups within the population as a whole and the factors that differentiate those subgroups (Rostek and Skala 2017).

In 2016, more observations were collected (536). The questionnaire consisted of 144 variables, of which 140 were used for the analysis. The

Table 2.8 Strengths and weaknesses of startup ecosystems in the Visegrád countries

Country	*Strengths*	*Weaknesses*
Czech Republic	The highest quality of life in the group High urbanisation rate High activity in the labour market High investment activity in the field of R&D High ratio of R&D specialists among all employees Strong e-commerce Leader in the Global Innovation Index High proportion of exporters among the startups Leader in patents and registration of trademarks	Low activity in the area of Startup Weekends Low share of VC as a source of funding Low funding from the public sector
Hungary	Investments in R&D dominated by the private sector High penetration of mobile technologies World-famous "unicorn": Prezi.com High activity of local VC funds	Slow economic growth The highest level of digital exclusion The lowest position in the Doing Business 2017 ranking The lowest popularity of the B2G model
Poland	Large country, high human and economic potential High domestic consumption The best software engineers in the world Leader in the Doing Business 2016 ranking Organised the most Startup Weekends Google Campus in Warsaw Four large startup centres High level of EU financing	The lowest level of investment in R&D Low patent activity of enterprises High levels of digital exclusion Low penetration of mobile technologies The lowest position in the GII
Slovakia	High level of economic growth The highest labour productivity Strong e-commerce market High export activity The largest share of women among the founders of the surveyed startups Crowdfunding the most popular among respondents in V4 countries	The highest unemployment

Source: Own material based on: (Beauchamp and Skala 2017)

data was subjected to segmentation analysis on the basis of differentiating variables but without indicating the superordinate variable (target variable) of the segmentation using three methods:

- cluster analysis—using correlations to construct the cluster matrix to carry out a two-step cluster analysis in the learning process and making the selection according to the criterion of the best variables,
- clustering—using centroids to identify clusters, using learning without internal standardisation and limiting the final number of clusters to four,
- self-organising Kohonen networks—using principal components to identify segments, spread for internal standardisation, batch learning, and limiting the number of segments to four.

The results indicated the most important subgroups within the surveyed population as a whole and the factors that differentiate those subgroups (Rostek and Skala 2017). A comparison of results between 2015 and 2016 was also made.

For each of the segmentation methods used, the first result of the process consisted of so-called differentiating features, that is, the most important variables used for segmentation performed by the given method on the selected data set. As three segmentation methods were used on two sets of data (2015 and 2016), six groups of differentiating variables were distinguished, consisting of 14 unique variables. From this set of variables, nine were initially selected, and then narrowed down to six variables. The frequency of segment differentiation was chosen as the selection criterion; in other words, the attributes that were most often repeated in the sets of differentiating variables obtained by different methods, and which, at the same time, described the largest number of defined segments. The following differentiating variables were included in this group:

- development stage (mature/early),
- operating in the business-to-business model: B2B (yes/no)
- hardware production (yes/no)
- export (yes/no);
- main funding source (internal/external);
- collaboration with the academia/science (yes/no).

The results of the 2015 study indicated the existence of three startup clusters:

- developing innovative startups,
- scaling innovative startups,
- mature companies.

Reanalysis of the 2015 data set and the inclusion of data from the subsequent study carried out in 2016 allowed for the extension of the conclusions, albeit with care due to not always comparable results. Firstly, two main factors that differentiate segments in both editions of the study were identified:

- products and services offered to businesses (B2B) or consumers (B2C),
- using external or own funding.
- Four further differentiating variables were subsequently added:
- collaboration with the academia/science,
- focusing production on software or hardware,
- stage of business development,
- export.

On the basis of differentiating characteristics, distinctive segments (clusters) of startups were identified, that is, clusters which receive the highest number of indications on the most important differentiating attributes:

- SG2a (22% of the population in 2015): mature B2C startups producing software, collaborating with academia/science, and benefiting from external funding;
- SG3a (17% of the population in 2015): mature B2B startups financed by external investors;
- SOM1a (21% of the population in 2015): mature B2B startups producing hardware, with external funding, collaborating with the academia;
- SG2b (24% of the population in 2016): beginner B2B startups that produce hardware, collaborate with academia/science, and use external financing;

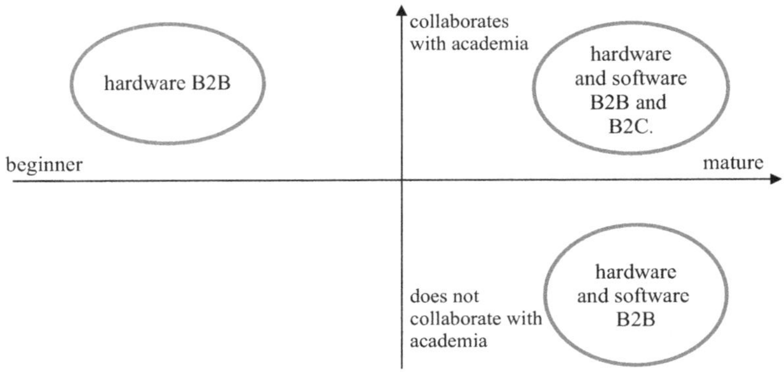

Fig. 2.1 Startup segments based on segmentation analysis. (Source: Own material)

- SG3b (27% of the population in 2016): mature B2B startups with external financing and not collaborating with the academia;
- SOM2b (16% of the population in 2016): beginner hardware startups, exporters, with external financing, and collaborating with the academia.

All startups belonging to these segments are backed by external financing, which can be seen as evidence of their high market potential as verified by investors and points to their advanced stage of development. Figure 2.1 maps three segments based on the main variables differentiating the studied population.

As a result of the research, three segments have been outlined in the population of the surveyed startups:

1. a homogeneous segment of beginner startups, producing hardware for business clients in collaboration with the academic/science sector;
2. a heterogeneous segment of mature startups collaborating with science, producing software or hardware for business or for individual customers;
3. a homogeneous segment of mature B2B startups not collaborating with the academia/science.

Thus, the three variables that differentiate the surveyed startups the most in 2015 and 2016 are:

- production in the B2B model,
- obtaining external financing,
- exports.

The relevance of the other two key differentiating variables, that is, hardware production and collaboration with the academia/science, will likely increase in the future much faster than the importance of the variables listed earlier. The presented analysis will be continued and improved in the subsequent editions of the "Polish Startups" study.

2.5 The Characteristics of Startups Using the "Spiral Definition of a Startup" and the Main Differentiating Variables

The results of the "Polish Startups" study are constructed in such a way that they allow for the visualisation of the data using the "startup spiral" proposed in Chap. 1 (Figs. 1.2 and 1.3) and for describing the startups using the main differentiating variables. Three non-overlapping sets of enterprises ("beginner", "fast-growing", and "mature") and one subset ("hyper-scalable", which belongs to the "mature" set) were isolated from the 2017 sample, based on the answers to selected questions from the questionnaire. The list of applied criteria and the size of thus obtained sets are presented in Table 2.9.

Beginner startups were at the first or the second stage of development, that is, developing and verifying the assumptions for their business model, team building, product development, prototyping, and acquiring the first customers and revenues (revenues cannot be regular). In addition, it was required that a beginner startup regularly interviewed its customers.

The fast-growing startups were at the second or third stage of development (a functioning business model, regular sales) and they had to report regular sales with a growth rate exceeding 20% per month (on average in the six months prior to the survey).

The mature startups indicated the advanced, fourth stage of development (expansion) and revenues exceeding 100,000 Polish zloty (approximately €23,000) per month (on average in the six months prior to the

Table 2.9 Startup groups according to the criteria used for division

Criteria		beginner	fast growing	mature	*including: hyper-scalable*
The entity is a startup		yes	yes	yes	yes
Stage of development	I	yes			
	II	yes	yes		
	III		yes		
	IV			yes	yes
The enterprise reports regular sales revenues			yes	yes	yes
The entity reports regular revenues above PLN 100,000 per month				yes	yes
The enterprise reports an average increase in sales above 20% / month.			yes		
The enterprise regularly interviews customers		yes			
Employs 20 or fewer people					yes
Population size		**180**	**152**	**50**	**21**

Source: Own material

survey). An additional condition fulfilled by hyper-scalable startups was employing not more than 20 people.

In this way, four groups of startups were defined, which were placed on the "startup spiral" (Fig. 2.2).

Next, each group was described with the five attributes that differentiate the startups the most: production in the B2B model, external funding, exports, hardware production, and collaboration with the academia/science (the last attribute was split into two variables: patent-related activity and collaboration with a science centre). Table 2.10 contains a numerical presentation of the attributes for all the groups, while a visualisation of this description is shown in Fig. 2.3.

Based on the analysis, a structured characteristic of the startups can be proposed:

- as expected, the beginners (180 entities) form the largest group, although the group at the further stage of development is only slightly smaller (150 entities);
- 50 enterprises have reached the mature stage, with 21 of those being hyper-scalable, as defined by a high ratio of revenue to employment (over PLN 5000/1 employee per month);

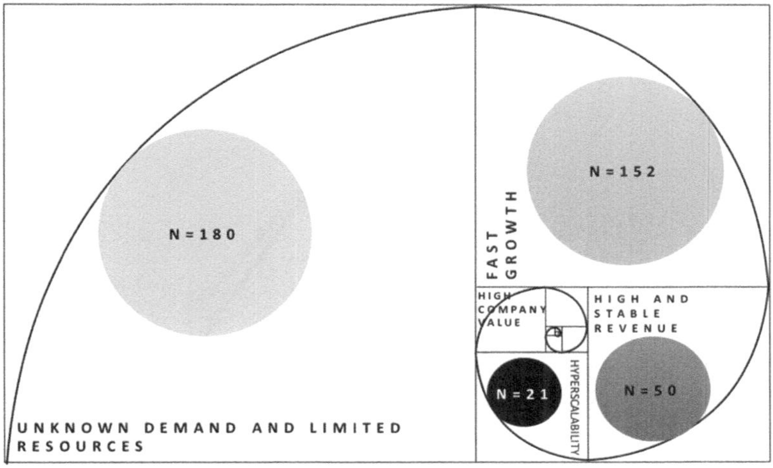

Fig. 2.2 Groups on the startup spiral, according to the "Polish Startups" study 2017. (Source: Own material)

Table 2.10 The percentage of startups reporting the main differentiating attributes in each group

Differentiating characteristics	*Startup group*			
	Beginners	*Fast-growing*	*Mature*	*Hyper-scalable*
B2B: business-to-business	78	85	84	86
Have external funding	29	58	56	50
Are exporting	33	65	92	91
Hardware producers	34	15	12	24
Collaborate with a science centre	56	39	44	43
Patent their solutions	23	11	22	24

Source: Own material

- in general, the B2B model predominates in all groups (84–86% of responses), with a slightly lower percentage only in the beginner group (78%);
- beginner startups most often collaborate with academic/research centres and most often manufacture hardware, while the lowest percentage of these decide to export; they use external financing rarely (less than one in three);

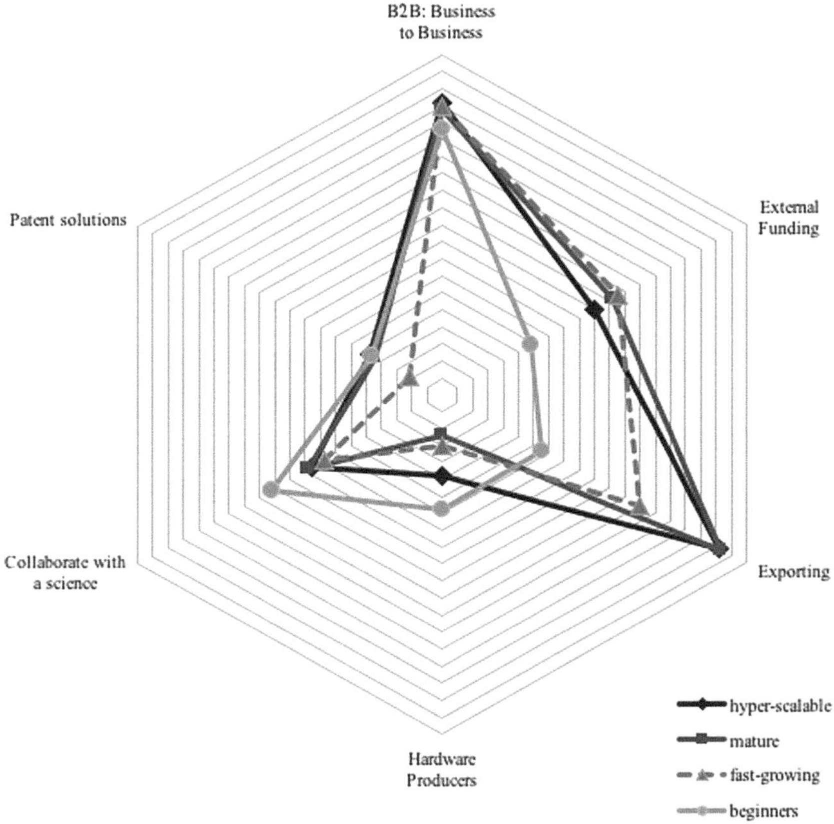

Fig. 2.3 Startups at various stages of development according to the main differentiating variables (% of the group reporting the attribute). (Source: Own material)

- the profile of fast-growing startups (it is worth remembering that this is a high rate of growth: at least 20% revenue increase per month) points to the focus of this group's efforts on gaining external financing and entering foreign markets (indicators in this respect twice as high than in the beginner group); the lowest share of enterprises that hold/apply for patents and half as frequent hardware production in comparison to the beginners are also noteworthy.

- the group of mature startups (with stable and high revenues) is characterised by a focus on exports (more than 90% of mature startups export) and, in a sense, a "second wave" of collaboration with academia/science, which also involves patenting their solutions;
- the group of hyper-scalable enterprises (mature with a particularly high employee productivity) is not very different from the mature group, apart from a few per cent drop in the proportion using external funding and a noticeably larger proportion of hardware producers in this group (every fourth hyper-scalable startup).

The analysis allowed for defining and describing four groups of enterprises, which are certainly startups in terms of the spiral definition, and which confirm the specificity at each of the defined stages of development. For example, the collaboration of startups with academia/science occurs in two "waves": when entering the market and at the mature stage; conquering foreign markets is a permanent process in the life of startups, while external funding is typical for startups at the rapid growth stage. This knowledge can be very useful both for planning the support structure for startups and for designing educational programmes.

2.6 Chapter Summary

Startups are more and more often the subject of interest for scientists, consulting companies, and state institutions which undertake to study and describe this group of enterprises. This is a difficult task mainly due to the unresolved issue of the definition of a startup, as well as due to the inconsistent methodology for conducting such research. Moreover, the official records listing enterprises are mostly useless for identifying startups. As a result, most of the published studies are fragmentary and, to a large extent, incomparable, which makes it difficult to carry out wider or in-depth analysis and makes it almost impossible to capture developmental trends. The intention of many research projects to date has been to determine the impact of startups on the economy on the regional or local scale; however, the fragmentary character of available data does not allow for making such estimates with scientific accuracy. In the light of problems with defining a startup, often entire startup ecosystems are treated as a research subject, as more easily identifiable phenomena, and ones with a wider, easier to quantify organisational and institutional reach.

The study of startups initiated and coordinated by the author and carried out by the Startup Poland Foundation since 2015 is of a pioneering character and provides significant research material. Although the four-year-long history of this project does not yet allow for developing far-reaching conclusions about the directions and dynamics of changes that digital industry startups undergo, each edition of the study gets closer to achieving the goal of determining the importance of startups for the economy. The high and growing number of surveyed enterprises and the fact that in more than 80% of the cases the questionnaire was completed by the key people in the company allow for a high degree of confidence in the collected results, despite the fact that the sample is not strictly statistically representative.

This chapter has described the study and presents an in-depth analysis of the results based on segmentation analysis and the spiral definition of a startup presented in Chap. 1. As a result, several groups of enterprises, which undoubtedly are startups, were identified in the whole studied population and described. In this way, four profiles of homogeneous groups of startups were obtained, with noticeably different goals depending on the stage of development. The knowledge about the changes in the business priorities can be very useful both in terms of various institutions planning a support structure for startups and for designing educational programmes in the process of educating future entrepreneurs.

The distinctive feature of startups is also their organisational culture, which manifests in the creation of open communities, diversity, and belonging to startup ecosystems. This culture has a global dimension, which is why it can be easily recognised in various places around the world, but it also fits within local entrepreneurship style to varying degrees. Startups derive important resources from their communities—knowledge, networks of contacts, and human resources—and they contribute to those communities in various ways, often acting "ahead of time", in accordance with the unwritten startup rule: "pay it forward" (i.e. "contribute something before you get something yourself"). This principle means that the organisation allocates its time and resources for the development of the community without expecting anything specific in return, guided by the belief that the benefits will sooner or later materialise and that the invested energy will return "with an extra on top". The startup communities are open, and the membership is free and voluntary. In the author's belief, this is a unique culture (even resembling some aspects of charity work or volunteering) in the landscape of Polish entrepreneurship, providing the participating organisations and people advantages, in terms of both individual entities and the entire industry. Because knowledge is one of the main resources shared within the community, certain specific methods, techniques, and even philosophies of startup management are particularly widespread in this community.

References

Alexy, O. T., Block, J. H., Sandner, P., & Ter Wal, A. L. (2012). Social capital of venture capitalists and start-up funding. *Small Business Economics, 39*(4), 835–851.

Autio, E. (1997). 'Atomistic' and 'systemic' approaches to research on new, technology-based firms: A literature study. *Small Business Economics, 9*(3), 195–209.

Badzińska, E. (2014). Indywidualizacja rozwiązań ICT w praktyce gospodarczej na przykładzie start-upów akademickich. *Informatyka Ekonomiczna, 2*(32), 24–32.

Badzińska, E. (2015). Determinanty rozwoju organizacji na przykładzie start-upu akademickiego. *Marketing i Rynek, 5*(CD), 708–722.

Beauchamp, M., & Skala, A. (2017). *Visegrád Startup Report 2016/2017.* Warszawa: Startup Poland.

Beauchamp, M., Kowalczyk, A., & Skala, A. (2017). *Polish Startups. Report 2017.* Warszawa: Startup Poland.

Beauchamp, M., Skala, A., & Krysztofiak-Szopa, J. (2018). *Polish Startups. Report 2018.* Warszawa: Startup Poland.

Block, J. H., Fisch, C. O., Hahn, A., & Sandner, P. G. (2015). Why do SMEs file trademarks? Insights from firms in innovative industries. *Research Policy, 44*(10), 1915–1930.

Bollinger, L., Hope, K., & Utterback, J. M. (1983). A review of literature and hypotheses on new technology-based firms. *Research Policy, 12*, 1–14.

Breschi, S. J., Lassébie, C., & Menon, C. (2018). *A portrait of innovative start-ups across countries* (OECD Science, Technology and Industry Working Papers). OECD.

Bursiak, L. (2013). Diagnoza i pozycjonowanie sytuacji nansowej firm start-up oraz spółek z rynku New-Connect w roku 2011. *Zeszyty Naukowe Uniwersytetu Szczecińskiego. Finanse. Rynki nansowe Ubezpieczenia, 760*(59), 49–58.

Bursiak, L. (2014). Dynamika kreacji firm start-up w wybranych krajach europejskich w latach 2007–2013. *Zeszyty Naukowe Zachodniopomorskiej Szkoły Biznesu Firma i Rynek, 2*, 5–16.

Burżacka, M., & Gąsiorowska, E. (2015). New Connect w nansowaniu działalności typu start-up. *Acta Universitatis Nicolai Copernici. Nauki Humanistyczno-Społeczne Zarządzanie, 42*(3), 163.

Calvino, F. C., Criscuolo, C., & Menon, C. (2016). *No country for young firms?: Start-up dynamics and national policies* (OECD Science, Technology and Industry Policy Papers no 29). Paris: OECD Publishing.

Cooper, A. C. (1971). *The founding of technologically-based firms.* Milwaukee: The Center for Venture Management.

Criscuolo, C., Gal, P. N., & Menon, C. (2014). *The dynamics of employment growth: New evidence from 18 countries* (OECD Science, Technology and Industry Policy Papers, no 14). Paris: OECD Publishing.

Cunha, D., Silva, S., & Teixeira, A. C. (2013). *Are academic spin-offs necessarily new technology-based firms* (Research Work in Progress), vol. 482.

Dalle, J., den Besten, M., & Menon, C. (2017). *Using Crunchbase for economic and managerial research* (OECD Science, Technology and Industry Working Papers, no 8). Paris: OECD Publishing.

Fontes, M., & Coombs, R. (2001). Contribution of new technology-based firms to the strengthening of techno-logical capabilities in intermediate economies. *Research Policy, 30*, 79–97.

Gemzik-Salwach, A. (2014a). Wpływ kryzysu światowego na rynek przedsiębiorstw start-up. *Acta Universitatis Lodziensis. Folia Oeconomica, 2*(300), 99–109.

Gemzik-Salwach, A. (2014b). *Wykorzystanie metody Dave'a Berkusa do analizy potencjału rozwojowego firm start-up w Polsce. Acta Universitatis Lodziensis. Folia Oeconomica, 2*(300), 111–122.

Gieżyńska, K., & Skala, A. (2016). Translating digital into high-tech economy. In K. Śledziewska (Ed.), *Digital ecosystems. Smart economy and innovation.* Warszawa: DELab UW.

Giones, F., & Brem, A. (2017). Digital technology entrepreneurship: A definition and research agenda. *Technology Innovation Management Review, 7*(5), 44–51.

Guzman J., & Stern S. (2016). *The state of American entrepreneurship: New estimates of the quantity and quality of entrepreneurship for 15 US States, 1988–2014* (National Bureau of Economic Research, Working Paper, no 22095).

Haltiwanger, J., Jarmin, R. S., & Miranda, J. (2013). Who creates jobs? Small versus large versus young. *Review of Economics and Statistics, 95*(2), 347–361.

Januszkiewicz, K. (2016). Od teorii naukowych do badania empirycznego – budowa narzędzi do badania zachowań ludzi w organizacji. *Przegląd Organizacji, 12*, 37–42.

Kelley, D., & Nakosteen, R. (2005). Technology resources, alliances and sustained growth in new, technology based firms. *IEEE Transactions on Engineering Management, 52*(3), 29–300.

Korpysa, J. (2012). Uwarunkowania przedsiębiorczości indywidualnej przedsiębiorstw typu start-up. *Studia Ekonomiczne Regionu Łódzkiego, 8*, 377–388.

Kruczkowska, E., & Skala, A. (2016). *Polish Startups. Report 2016.* Warszawa: Startup Poland.

Kruczkowska, E., Olczak, M., & Skala, A. (2015). *Polish Startups. Report 2015.* Warszawa: Startup Poland.

Laranja, M., & Fontes, M. (1998). Creative adaptation: The role of new technology based firms in Portugal. *Research Policy, 26*, 1023–1036.

Rostek, K., & Skala, A. (2014). Differentiating criteria for high-tech companies. *Management and Production Engineering Review, Polska Akademia Nauk – Komitet Inżynierii Produkcji, 5*(4), 46–52.

Rostek, K., & Skala, A. (2017). Differentiating criteria and segmenting Polish startup companies. *Problemy Zarządzania, 1*, 65.

Rothwell, R. (1989). Small firms, innovation and industrial change. *Small Business Economics, 1*, 51–64.

Santisteban, J., & Mauricio, D. (2017). Systematic literature review of critical success factors of information technology startups. *Academy of Entrepreneurship Journal, 23*(2), 1–23.

Skala, A. (2014). Nowa metoda identyfikacji przedsiębiorstw wysokiej technologii na przykładzie Warszawy. *Modern Management Review, XIX*(21(2)), 109–127.

Storey, D. J., & Tether, B. S. (1998). New technology-based firms in the European Union: An introduction. *Research Policy, 26*, 933–946.

Wong, P., Ho, Y., & Autio, E. (2005). Entrepreneurship, innovation and economic growth: Evidence from GEM data. *Small Business Economics, 24*(3), 335–350.

World Bank. (2017). *Doing Business.* http://www.doingbusiness.org/reports/global-reports/doing-business-2017. Accessed 30 Mar 2018.

CHAPTER 3

Startups as a Challenge for Management and Education

Abstract This chapter presents a new philosophy of startup management—Lean Startup—in the context of management culture. Particular attention is placed on the development of management in Poland, including historical and social factors. The technocratic spirit of large manufacturing industry and the tradition of family businesses and small-scale artisan production clash with the startup culture which is open, egalitarian, and dynamic, but also nomadic and volatile. These attributes of startup culture are a source of its strength and potential, but they can be a barrier to its rapid adaptation in Poland and other countries with similar experiences. The second part of the chapter is devoted to education for startups in the context of education in the field of management and entrepreneurship. The chapter also presents examples of the author's own courses programmes educating for startup entrepreneurship based on her knowledge and experience conducting classes and training for students and entrepreneurs.

Keywords Change • Startup management • Lean Startup • Education for startups

Management, in line with the theory developed since the mid-nineteenth century, involves sequential operation according to the following model:

A. Skala, *Digital Startups in Transition Economies*,
https://doi.org/10.1007/978-3-030-01500-8_3

planning, organising, recruitment, management, coordinating, reporting, and budgeting.[1] Formalised management is, however, constantly questioned by the practice of management work, which is actually much more chaotic than the theory stipulates. The cognitive gap between theory and practice is an important inspiration for management research; it is its subject, and as a result contributes to the developments in this area. The methodology of managing a startup poses a significant conceptual challenge because proven, and theoretically well-established, "traditional" methods of enterprise management do not work for startups. This chapter attempts to answer questions about the impact of startups on management, and about the distinctive nature of managing startups. The subject of consideration in this chapter is the new Lean Startup management methodology, which has been developed "by startups for startups" and which responds to their needs. The chapter will also consider whether this methodology is scientific and to what extent, and, following from this, its importance for management science.

Management education is a particularly important element of entrepreneurship ecosystems, because it shapes the main development factor in these ecosystems—the human factor. Education for startups (in other words, for the benefit of startups) is an element of management education sensu *largo*. The dilemmas of management and entrepreneurship education are thus also related to the training of startup founders and other members of a broadly defined startup ecosystem. The discrepancy between the theory of management and management practice, including business, and the problematic attitude of scientific authorities and educational institutions towards new management concepts such as Lean Startup have a direct impact on educational design and content, and, importantly, they can lead to serious discrepancies between formal and informal education. In the second part of the chapter, a review of the copious, but fairly new and not yet well-established literature on the subject will be made. The main directions for research and current challenges in this area will be discussed, followed by the presentation of selected examples of the implementation of proprietary education programmes.

[1] POSDCORB: *Planning, Organizing, Staffing, Directing, Co-ordinating, Reporting, Budgeting.*

3.1 Contemporary Challenges for Management

Vlatka Hlupic, a recognised British thinker in the field of innovative management and the author of *The Management Shift* (Hlupic 2014), believes that there has never been such a great need to change how we think about management sensu *largo* as there is now. Hlupic believes that contemporary organisations suffer from the "boiled frog syndrome" (Hlupic 2017), that is, satisfied with themselves and unconscious of the imminent danger, they do not make necessary changes, which will soon prove fatal to them. Meanwhile, as Hlupic claims, the existing business management paradigms do not fit the new market landscape. More and more often, companies operate globally, which is possible thanks to unprecedented progress in the field of communication and digitisation. Markets are transforming, and demographic changes affect team management methods, marketing, and leadership. This also means that the competitor profiles are constantly evolving, and that the emphasis on innovation, collaboration, and cooperation between organisations is growing. Organisations that follow a path based on such values as honesty, empathy, permanent innovation, and the commitment to a "positive changing of the world for future generations" are becoming more and more adapted to the new reality. Hlupic defines the need for this change as "dramatic", as many organisations, both in the public and in the private sectors, must make deep systemic transformations in relation to not only management practices but also their organisational culture, business processes, regulatory framework, organisation, and work ethic. Startups are one of the manifestations and an emanation of those changes.

As a result of rapid technical progress, in particular the development of the Internet, companies gained universal access to resources or markets that would be out of their reach even 30 years ago. New opportunities and business models emerged, and one of the main areas of theoretical research is conditions for the creation and development of innovative and dynamically developing enterprises. Leading entrepreneurship researchers (Shane and Venkataraman 2000) discuss its role, place, and importance among management sciences and the challenges its undoubted renaissance brings (Cieślik 2014a, 2015, 2017; Kurczewska 2013). The main areas in the ongoing debate include:

- the impact of dematerialisation and virtualisation of the economy on enterprises; Beata Glinka and Monika Kostera (2012) present, on the one hand, new opportunities for increasing productivity, creating new organisational structures, and better meeting customer needs and, on the other hand, problems related to the collection, processing, and use of a huge amount of information, and complex legal issues regarding intellectual property management. As intangible factors become more and more important for building a competitive advantage, new methods for managing not only those resources but also the entire enterprise are required (Adamczyk 2016). The results of the analysis of huge data sets (*Big Data*) are more and more often used to support decision-making, also excluding human participation, which in consequence means the automation of some management functions and, ultimately, a change in the role of managers in organisations (Łada 2016);

- redefinition of the purpose of doing business, because the one that seemed obvious so far, that is, maximising the benefits to company shareholders, has been devalued. The 2007 financial crisis undermined confidence in business sensu *largo* and stimulated a discussion not so much about finances as about trust, morality, greed, and contempt for other market participants. Works which undermine the foundations of modern economics are being widely discussed (Piketty 2014) and suggest that broadly understood social needs be included in the cost/benefit analysis of private companies (Reiser 2011). These suggestions are based on specific data—research shows that socially responsible companies attract better staff, more loyal customers, and more generous investors, compared to companies that do not take into account the social aspect of their activities (see Batra et al. 2012; Dhaliwal et al. 2011; Backhaus et al. 2002). According to a PricewaterhouseCoopers report (2014), more than two-thirds of CEOs believe that their company's goal is to balance the benefits for all stakeholders—not just the owners of the enterprise;
- new expectations towards managers; for example, in Poland a strong link between an engineer and a manager is a fact—the research conducted annually by *Rzeczpospolita* daily shows that the percentage of technical university graduates among CEOs of the largest Polish companies is approximately 45–50% (Błaszczak and Ogonowska-Rejer 2016). And although this percentage has been consistently decreasing, still no other professional group is as strongly represented among managers as engineers are. Engineering education is

characterised by the logical order of construction, technology, and operation and prepares the ground for easily adopting the principles of organisational order. This tradition thus facilitates reliable operations, but on the other hand, it favours pragmatic attitudes over creativity and broad visions. Meanwhile, management is currently undergoing greater humanisation. Research on the impact of overall management quality on economic growth (Koźmiński 2014) has shown that the so-called soft factors, especially the dissemination of modern management methods, are very important in this process. According to Steve Blank (2016), only balancing both attitudes—the pragmatic and the visionary—gives a chance for achieving success and maintaining the position of a market leader, especially in technology, while managers too strongly focused on immediate results (which they, often with a spectacular success, achieve) lose sight of a long-term strategy. Blank cites the example of Microsoft, which, after Bill Gates's "abdication" in 2000, achieved impressive financial results under Steve Ballmer's helm for the following 14 years, tripling sales and doubling profits. Nevertheless, at the same time, the company lost its position in the five most important growth areas of the ICT market: search engine technologies (to Google), smartphones (to Apple), mobile operating systems (to Google and Apple), media (to Apple and Netflix), and cloud services (to Amazon). Pushing creative and strategic attitudes on the back burner in favour of short-term profitability is particularly dangerous for listed companies, for whom a frequent reporting obligation rewards stability and repetitive processes over vision and innovation;
- distancing the theory and teaching of management from business practice (see Nicholas et al. 2011; David et al. 2011), which manifests itself in limited cooperation between both communities and a lack of mutual trust (Zawiła-Niedźwiecki 2014), and even contempt towards scientific works drawing inspiration from practice, perceived as less valuable (Chrostowski and Jemielniak 2008). As a result, new business solutions are often developed by commercial consulting companies, not universities or research institutes.

The tradition of scientific management, according to which management methods and techniques mainly serve to increase the efficiency of work and the use of other resources, on the one hand created management as a scientific discipline, but on the other, it can be a barrier to its further development. The organisation is now perceived as a "living" organism, constantly evolving and, therefore, difficult to permanently model (cf. Clegg et al. 2017). In the "liquid modernity" described by Zygmunt Bauman (Bauman and Kunz 2006) and Manuel Castells (Castells and Marody 2013), organisations have neither the time nor the need to create permanent structures because their main goal is to achieve extreme flexibility and permanent alertness in relation to an uncertain, episodic, and "fluid" environment. Therefore, a question arises: to what extent the achievements of the main schools of management fits the needs of effective management of an innovative, ambitious enterprise?

3.2 The Tradition of Management in Poland

The tradition of management in Poland has its roots in two sources. The first is the classic trends originating in the large manufacturing industry and production engineering (cf. Czech 2004), with notable works by Karol Adamiecki, Edwin Hauswald, and Aleksander Rothert. The few cases of successful Polish enterprises operating during the partitions period (1795–1918) are an example of the success of changes that had been implemented for decades in the period before independence, and which were definitely incremental and sporadic in nature (Wodecka-Hyjek 2013). Put simply, they were a deviation from the rule, because the objective of the partitioning powers' economic policy was to plunge the occupied Polish areas in economic backwardness, which was implemented especially by the Russian partitioner in the second half of the nineteenth century, after the January Uprising (1863). This policy did not even bypass locations like the "promised land" in Łódź, where industrial factories were built in spite of the glaringly inadequate infrastructural conditions that prevailed there—and this refers to technical, municipal, and transport infrastructure, as well as to social infrastructure, for example, seriously underdeveloped education. More than a century during which Poland lacked statehood had a clearly negative impact on entrepreneurship, but, on the other hand, it forced people interested in business careers to seek knowledge, inspiration, and financing abroad, where they had the opportunity to encounter much more mature industrialised economies. From the point of view of the problems discussed in this publication, two issues seem particularly important in this context. The first is the linking of the management tradition with the big manufacturing industry, which often resulted in merging management and engineering competences. Secondly, no significant class of entrepreneurs with substantial financial capital and managerial experience emerged in Poland in the described conditions, and the intense yet short interwar period of independence (1918–1939) was not sufficient to make up for such huge losses.

The second trend of modern management culture emerged in Poland with the spontaneous entrepreneurship of the 1990s, when the long-restricted Polish entrepreneurship exploded on the wave of political transformation (the so-called Wilczek Act, i.e. the "legendary" Act on economic activity of 1989.[2]) At the same time, it is worth noting, what Jerzy Cieślik consistently emphasises in his work, that even in the times of a centrally planned economy (1945–1989), Poland remained an exception among the Eastern Bloc countries in that small-scale entrepreneurship, especially from the 1970s onwards, existed here—although within a narrow and strictly controlled framework (cf. Cieślik 2006, 2014b, 2017). However, the non-market and irrational conditions in which the *prywaciarze* (small-scale entrepreneurs of the communist era) functioned at that time meant that their experience turned out to be useless in the new economic reality after 1989. The continuity of the short and fragile entrepreneurship tradition was again interrupted, and the pre-war generation was by then already in retirement.

When the previously mentioned *Act on economic activity* entered into force (1989), Poles, regardless of their resources and social class, began to set up small companies en masse (often having no other choice because of the closures of state enterprises and group layoffs after 1990) and developed them, relying much more on intuition and common sense than on knowledge and skills (which everyone lacked). Both the good and the bad sides of a rapid socio-economic transformation in the conditions of fledgling democracy, rampant capitalism, and disturbed social structures became apparent in this process. It was then that the myth of very quick and easy earnings arose, as well as links between business and crime, while the awkwardness of the emerging free market structures and state institutions placed business and the state on the opposite sides of the mental "barricade" for many years. The Poles persisted in their belief, dating to the times of partitions (1798–1918), the wartime occupation (1939–1945), and the centrally planned economy (1945–1989), that money **could not** be earned uprightly. This thread is also raised by B. Glinka (2008), who on the basis of her own research on Polish attitudes towards the phenomenon of entrepreneurship concluded

[2] Act of 23 December 1988 on economic activity. Dz.U. 1988 No. 41 item 324.

that the approval for entrepreneurial attitudes in Poland is fairly modest, and the more successful and bigger the enterprise, the lower the approval. Small-scale entrepreneurs of the artisan type enjoy greater approval, perceived as men of hard, honest, and arduous work. In other words, the more traditional the entrepreneurship the greater social acceptance it enjoys, and the more it shows innovation, creativity, and momentum the less it's approved of. This is an important thread in the context of startups, because entrepreneurship mentality and business culture that were shaped especially strongly in the period of systemic transformation are still an important barrier to a more intensive development of innovative, ambitious, and dynamic forms of entrepreneurship in Poland and other transition countries in the region.

3.3 Startups as a Challenge for Management

Management as a scientific discipline has been, on the one hand, created by the tradition of scientific management and the neoclassical approach to business, according to which the ultimate goal of the existence of the enterprise is to provide benefits to its owners, while management methods and techniques mainly serve to increase efficiency of work and the use of other resources. On the other hand, these traditions constitute one of the most important challenges management science faces. The tradition is so strong that to this day, among both theorists and practitioners of management, there is a widespread belief that there is one just form and method for organising work, the use of which maximises the results. This approach has been subjected to criticism for some time, as organisations are now perceived as "living" organisms, constantly evolving and, therefore, not subject to permanent modelling (cf. Clegg et al. 2017). It is worth asking the question here: do current achievements of the main schools of management correspond to the needs of effective startup management?

In the context of the challenges discussed in the previous subsection, some serious doubts arise. The main tool for planning a new venture is a business plan—a document with a fixed structure.

> After the initial examination of the market, the future entrepreneur begins to collect resources—mostly financial, but also material and human. Then they formally register the company and the project enters its start-up phase, which in the case of technologically advanced projects can be several months or even several years long. Only when products and technological processes pass the feasibility tests, the promotion of the company and its new products on the market begins. (Cieślik 2015, p. 64)

This is a commonly used approach, also for project management within larger organisations, where ideas are developed internally. Meanwhile, in relation to innovative ventures, especially those developed in new markets, where products and services are often non-material (virtual), business plans do not work as a method for organising work and management (cf. Blank 2013; Sommer et al. 2009; Lange et al. 2007). Entrepreneurs begin operations under conditions of high uncertainty, where there are so many unknowns that accurately predicting events and estimating main business parameters (revenues, costs, sales volume) is impossible. The answer to such situation is, for example, the concept of agile management of projects or whole enterprises (Trzcieliński 2011). Only a larger, stable company that implements a known business model can afford long-term planning. In the case of a startup, this situation does not occur, because a startup is still looking for its model of operations (i.e. its business model) and this is the fundamental difference between a startup and a stable company established in the market (see Chap. 1). In other words, when a company determines its business model, that is, it knows the mechanisms that allow it to earn from the value proposition it sells to its clients, it stops being a startup and can start to "predict the future" by creating plans or using other business indicator forecasts.

In the case of innovative, especially technological, companies operating in volatile environments, planning in the form of a business plan usually does not lead to the expected results (primarily risk reduction) (cf. Tanev 2017; Picken 2017a). What's more, research shows that the launch phase is followed by an even more critical phase, so-called transition (Picken 2017a), in business jargon often called the "valley of death". In this relatively short period (usually 18–36 months) the founding team must lay the foundations for a rapidly growing business: build its credibility and provide the resources necessary for development. The requirements for experience and competencies required of the management team dramatically increase (Wasserman 2003). The founders must simultaneously deal with product development, market acquisition and sales strategy, team building, acquiring resources, shaping organisational culture, and risk management. The increased scope and complexity of activities requires the founding team to develop an acceptable style of leadership as well as other behaviours related to people management (Picken 2017b). The entrepreneur at this stage needs tools to develop the business model, which means learning the needs and preferences of the end customers, to develop a value proposition for which those customers will be willing to pay and which will be delivered to them in the form of a competitive product or service. A good business model, that is, the way the business operates, should also determine how relationships with customers are established and define sales channels, distribution, revenue model and operations, processes and partnerships accompanying the implementation of all of these activities (Johnson et al. 2008).

Founding a startup does not thus mean writing a plan, and then hiring people and entrusting them with tasks, although such a model used to occur and can still be popular. It is a reflection of the so-called waterfall (cascade) management model, proposed by Winston Royce (1987) for software development projects—where it is still used. However, the waterfall management model does not work long-term for business ventures, because there is a significant discrepancy between the art of developing IT products and launching them on the market. The popularity of "waterfall" management models is also the result of the previously discussed "melding" of engineering and management competences, because in technology-related startups the same people often deliver products and manage projects, or even the entire company. Programmers, taught how to deal with an IT project, have for years used the same models and procedures to found and run their businesses. Meanwhile, a startup does not know its business model but is searching for it and should focus its efforts on this search. The epochal challenge for management theory is therefore to provide models, tools, and techniques for managing a startup that will facilitate and speed up the process of searching for a business model at the lowest possible cost. It is in response to these challenges that the concept of the Lean Startup methodology was created.

3.4 Lean Startup as a Proposal for the Methodology of Managing Startup Development

Based on previous considerations, it can be concluded that:

1. startups appeared as specific forms of organisation that function within a specific institutional and cultural ecosystem and for this reason they need to develop a new, practical approach to managing them;

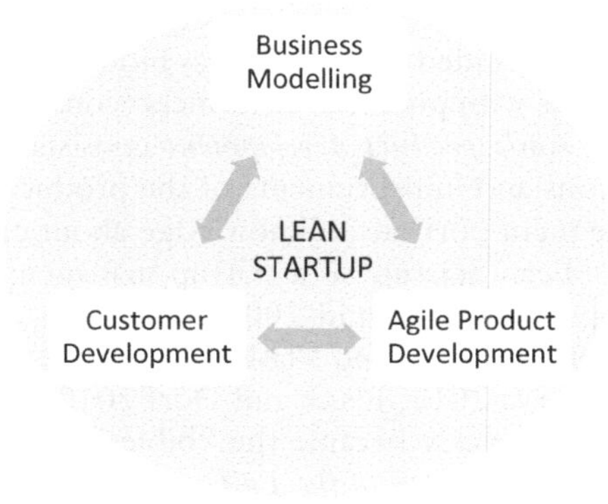

Fig. 3.1 Components of the Lean Startup methodology. (Source: Own material)

2. management theory and practice face fundamental challenges, among which the most important from the point of view of startups are those related to knowledge management and technological progress, extreme market volatility, and multicultural environments; challenges also appear within organisations that move away from hierarchical structures towards agile and flat solutions.

In response to these challenges, a specific management approach has been proposed: Lean Startup. This is, broadly speaking, a new organisation management methodology, which consists of three main tools (Fig. 3.1.):

1. customer development,
2. business modelling,
3. agile product development.

Business modelling means that instead of planning and conducting marketing research, the entrepreneur assumes that they have a set of unconfirmed hypotheses and assumptions, which they structure in the form of a business model, using the so-called canvas (Lean Canvas or Business Model Canvas [BMC]) or the Value Proposition Canvas; the concept of canvas graphically illustrates the business model, that is, the way in which the company creates and delivers value to the customer and monetises this value for its own benefit.

Customer development is the process of iterative verification of hypotheses included in the business model. It is carried out through direct interviews with potential customers (consumers).

Agile product development consists in iterative and gradual modifications and improvements of the product as the function of acquiring subsequent portions of knowledge about customers' problems and needs.

Lean Startup[3] as a startup management methodology has been developed since the mid-2000s by various authors (Blank 2003; Osterwalder 2004; Cooper and Vlaskovits 2010; Furr and Ahlstrom 2011; Ries 2011; Maurya 2012; Blank and Dorf 2012). Some particularly relevant publications quickly became the "bibles" for entrepreneurs using Lean Startup: *The Four Steps to the Epiphany* (Blank 2003), *Business Model Generation* (Osterwalder and Pigneur 2010), *The Lean Startup* (Ries 2011) and, finally, the summary *The Startup Owner's Manual* (Blank and Dorf 2012). Not all of them applied uniform nomenclature and consistent definitions, which is causing a certain level of conceptual chaos. The concept set out by Steve Blank is the best structured one, consistently applying the terminology defined by the author, and will therefore form the core of the description presented below.

In his publications and numerous public speeches, Steve Blank describes the sources of the Lean Startup concept and discusses the reasons for its success in the business community. The starting point is the truism that new ventures have always been created, and always with varying results. However, throughout the twentieth century, a startup was managed as if it were a "small version of a large company"—as Blank calls it. In his groundbreaking work *The Four Steps to the Epiphany* (2003), Blank concludes that such thinking was fundamentally mistaken, and that startups need to develop different management methods of their own, and that apart from MBA courses for managers in corporations, separate courses should be developed for startup founders. One of the most important consequences of Blank's thesis was the departure from the business plan as a basic management tool used by both investors and entrepreneurs themselves. Acquiring funds for this plan, or investing own funds, resulted in the transition to the stage of developing a product that was created "behind closed doors" and only in the final, usually much more elaborate

[3] So far, there is no satisfactory Polish translation for this term, so the original term will be used: "Lean Startup".

than the original idea version, hit the market, and reached the customer. Only at this stage the entrepreneur received the first feedback about the actual needs of consumers and their opinions about the new product, which often ended with a spectacular failure of the whole venture.

Lean Startup is a method of managing a new business venture that meets the first condition of the spiral definition of a startup: it enters the market where it encounters uncertainty or lack of demand for its product (or does not have a well-elaborated idea of what the product will eventually be) and has very limited resources, especially material resources. What a startup has is a business hypothesis about an observed market need, in other words a problem that a specific group of consumers encounters and which the startup intends to solve by delivering its product or service. This hypothesis should be verified at the stage of searching for a business model, iterating subsequent versions of the product and the model in line with the data incoming on an ongoing basis from the customers.

Currently, many existing barriers to the development of technological enterprise are disappearing: one can design, test, and deliver a product in a few weeks, not months, at one-hundredth or one-thousandth of what it would have costed 10–20 years ago. Not only huge high-risk capital funds invest in digital business, but also niche, "boutique" VC investors, accelerators, business angels, and corporations; there is also crowdsourcing. Access to information has a new, democratic character, as exemplified by the dynamic development and growth of the importance of startup communities as agents and spaces for sharing knowledge and experience (cf. Feld 2012; van Weele et al. 2014), as well as the popularity of open training courses in the MOOC (massive open online course) formula.

Nowadays, Lean Startup is implemented by global corporations (e.g. General Electric) in their development departments, where they search for and develop new business models—that is, they act as startups (Power 2014). This challenge requires them to acquire new skills and improve organisational structures. In recent years, management experts such as Clayton Christensen (Christensen and Raynor 2013), Rita McGrath (2013) with Ian MacMillan (1995, 2009), Vijay Govindarajan (Govindarajan and Ramamurti 2011), Henry Chesbrough (2006, 2010), Alexander Osterwalder (2004; Osterwalder and Pigneur 2010), and Eric von Hippel (2005) developed thinking on how big companies can improve their innovation processes.

Discussion of Lean Startup as a Methodology for Managing a Startup

Lean Startup was born in the community of programmers and entrepreneurs in the digital industry in the mid-2000s in the Silicon Valley. After several years, when the methodology gained recognition in its own community, it began to spread and adapt to other organisations and industries. The impact of Lean Startup on the development of entrepreneurship and its form is difficult to estimate today, but one can assume that it is significant, if not decisive (cf. Blank 2013). Lean Startup has changed the language that entrepreneurs use to describe their work. Terms like pivot, hypothesis, business modelling, product-market fit, or minimum viable product (MVP) have entered business language for good. Stealthy and secret activities have been replaced with openness to constructive criticism from the first days of the project, which is the driving force for the use of iterative and agile techniques for the development of products and services. Lean Startup is used by startups, corporations (Owens and Fernandez 2014), and national governments (United States, Finland), which create special programmes for funding startups, and the highest-ranking state officials open or organise the most important startup events (in Israel, in Finland, and also in Poland). Entrepreneurship education programmes for startups are introduced by the best universities and business schools in the world.

Meanwhile, scientific literature on Lean Startup is modest, even in the United States (cf. Teece 2010). It was not until 2015 that the first article on the Lean Startup methodology (Ladd et al. 2015) appeared in the most prestigious scientific journal on management in the United States, *Academy of Management*. Two years earlier, the *Harvard Business Review* had published the first article by Steve Blank (2013) about Lean Startup and made it the leading article for the entire issue. In 2016, Springer published post-conference materials in the form of a book in which one of the chapters was devoted to the methodology (Lago et al. 2016). Reviewing the bibliography of that chapter, it is worth noting that it does not contain a single item of conventional scientific literature, but includes numerous items published in *Harvard Business Review*, *Forbes* magazine, and books by Blank, Ries, and Osterwalder.

Ted Ladd, a professor of entrepreneurship and researcher at the Center for Disruptive Innovation at Hult International Business School, is the author of a few papers on Lean Startup (2016) in which he described studies in which he verified the effectiveness of this management methodology. Ladd analysed the results of 248 startup teams that participated in a year-long acceleration programme. The startups solved social and environmental problems, using digital technologies for this purpose.

The conclusions from the research confirm the main assumptions of the Lean Startup methodology. First of all, it was proved that personal interaction of founders with customers improves the effectiveness of a venture. It is not only about verification of business hypotheses, but also about a deeper, psychological effect. Namely, the "getting out of the building" by the founders, usually the originators of the startup, to interact with customers at the early stage of a project makes their approach to the original startup concept significantly more flexible, in the sense of not postponing the decisions on the necessary changes that result from the interviews. Ladd also showed that teams that set out and test hypotheses achieve better financial results after a time and do better in competitions for startups (such competitions can often result in additional funding for a startup). Ladd's research, however, did not show a correlation between the number of tested hypotheses and better results, that is, it is not the quantity that matters here. Thus, a limited number of hypotheses regarding key elements of the business model at the initial stage of the startup's development are sufficient to significantly improve the chances of the venture's success.

At the same time, Ladd clearly separates "experiment" from "interaction" with customers and the results of his research show substitution not

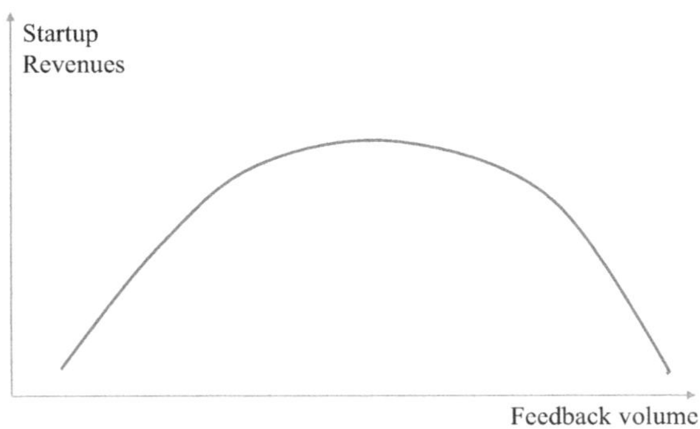

Fig. 3.2 The relationship between the results of the startup and the volume of feedback. (Source: Own material based on Ladd et al. 2015)

complementarity (as Blank and other creators of the concept assumed) between these two techniques. In other words, entrepreneurs who use both techniques simultaneously achieve less improvement in the results than those who apply them separately. Thus, too much interaction at one time, Ladd claims, is more likely to hinder entrepreneurs than help them, as it distracts from more effective actions. Ladd calls this phenomenon erosion of the startup's founders of trust in the customers, caused by the feeling of obtaining an excess of diverse opinions. Ladd hypothesises the existence of a reversed U-curve effect in this relationship, that is, after exceeding the critical mass of feedback, the improvement in the company's results loses its dynamics and then reverses (Fig. 3.2).

The phenomenon that Ladd noticed and described matches the observations of startups surveyed in Chap. 2. This is a typical problem that the founders (managers) of a startup face: postponing the moment of closing a given consultation stage, making the right decisions, and moving on in the process of venture development. This is a problem of a psychological nature, often associated with the difficulty in accepting or even the inability to accept that many consumer segments are simply not the customers of the startup, at least for now. Ladd's research clearly indicated that startups that focused their tests mainly on precisely defining their clients, value propositions, and channels for its delivery ("funnels") achieved significantly better results than those that focused their activities on other elements of the business model.

David Collis (2016), a Harvard Business School professor, noted in his discussion of the Lean Startup methodology in *HBR* that strategy and entrepreneurship are seen as opposites: strategy as moving towards clearly defined goals along a specific path and through a carefully selected set of actions; entrepreneurship as the personification of nonconformity, requiring atypical, diverse, often spontaneous actions in response to fast-changing market data. Collins believes that despite these differences, the two attitudes are complementary, because strategy without entrepreneurship equals central planning, and entrepreneurship without strategy results in chaos. Meanwhile, strategy sets the limits within which innovations appear and experiments are made. Collins puts forward the thesis that the Lean Startup methodology, which he calls Lean Strategy, offers a chance to reconcile those seemingly contradictory elements, both for startups, where the lack of strategy threatens with dispersal of ideas and limited resources, and for large companies in which strategic management stifles innovation and organisational complexity limits creative interactions between people.

Another issue discussed in the context of the Lean Startup methodology is its scientific nature and grounding in the theory of management or entrepreneurship. This question was addressed by professors of the Syddansk University in Denmark: Dennis L. Frederiksen and Alexander Brem (2017), who carried out a critical analysis of Eric Ries's book *Lean Startup*. These authors claimed that Ries took a certain shortcut in his justifying the legitimacy of the principles on which he had based the Lean Startup philosophy exclusively with case studies (mainly from his own career) and expert opinions. They analysed the subject literature, searching for scientific evidence supporting the truth (or demonstrating the falsity) of Ries's assumptions. That search proved fruitful, despite the strong polemical tone of the authors' argument towards Ries's publication. The authors distinguished five main principles (elements) of Lean Startup and assessed their grounding in science.

Referring to the first element, the authors found strong arguments confirming the positive impact of the so-called open innovation on the results (including financial results) in enterprises that apply and use it in their innovative activities, especially when creating new products. Comprehensive research on this subject means that the theory is very well backed by research.

The same applies to the iterative methods of product development—a reference to iterative software development (the so-called XP) has already been cited in the literature (Gassmann et al. 2006) as one which guarantees that unpromising projects are revealed quickly and with low expenses incurred for their development. A rich empirical study of innovative projects using the so-called process with parallel actions, which copies the iterative approach proposed by Ries, was also described by Salerno et al. (2015) and Becker et al. (2015). The latter additionally argued that this method is also appropriate for enterprises outside the software industry.

The third area, "experimentation", is the first in which the amount of available literature was considered unsatisfactory. According to Ries, the uncertainty facing a startup speaks in favour of experimenting, so in the face of the huge deficit of verified facts, knowledge must be generated through action and experimentation. Frederiksen and Brem cite Thomke (1998), who proposed the so-called learning cycle, with a structure very similar to Ries's build-measure-learn loop. Sykes and Dunham (1995) make a similar reference in the form of "critical planning". Thomke conducted detailed, large-scale empirical studies that showed a significant increase in performance with a growing number of iterations and experiments (2003). However, Hauser et al. (2006) called for in-depth research on this issue, especially in the context of various non-software industries. Finally, Andries et al. (2013) interpreted experimentation as a way of dealing with uncertainty, exactly as proposed by Ries, and confirmed that it increased the chances for long-term survival.

The fewest literature references were found in relation to the MVP concept, of which a large proportion were secondary publications referring to Ries himself. On the other hand, the fifth element—effectuation (Sarasvathy 2001, 2008)—and the notion of "unsuitability of planning for conditions of high uncertainty" find strong backing in research. Lange et al. (2007) studied the impact of creating a business plan on the subsequent results of the venture and obtained negative results (like Sommer et al. 2009 later).

In their summary, Frederiksen and Brem conclude that the key elements of the Lean Startup methodology have significant backing in literature. This evidence is not particularly substantial for designing experiments and setting business hypotheses—the main component of the methodology—so more in-depth research on this topic will provide a better understanding of the whole concept of Lean Startup. Moreover, as results of such experiments have a major impact on management decisions (previously mentioned "pivots", i.e. significant changes in the business model), special attention should be paid to designing those experiments to be reliable and methodologically sound, and at the same time ensuring they can still be realistically conducted in conditions of high uncertainty. Finally, the authors not only admit that Lean Startup explains how entrepreneurs create value but also admit that using this methodology significantly contributes to effective delivery of value to customers. Nevertheless, the authors do not see a potential for a wide application of Lean Startup in companies outside digital industries sensu *stricte*.

Is Lean Startup already a school or just a fad in management sciences? Wojciech Czakon (2014) says that

> when a community shares a common identity, and recognises one or several leading lights whose ideas are developed over a longer period, one can talk about a scientific school. (…) On the other hand, if a research community is formed under external pressure, as with the phenomenon of growing attractiveness due to a growing popularity, then its cohesion is not rooted in shared principles, identity or a 'master'. On the contrary, the source of cohesion is the fashionable trend, soon to be replaced by another fad. The fashion should be followed, so as not to risk a decline in attractiveness.

> Interestingly, researchers follow scientific fashions not any less than managers do. It's managers who create fashions and contribute to the rapid growth of popularity of a given approach, technique or concept. On the other hand, in the long run the researchers contribute to the decline in the popularity of a fashion until its fading.

On this basis, it is difficult to give an unambiguous answer to the question posed earlier. However, more and more scientific papers cover Lean Startup, and its "gurus" are more and more often invited to key scientific and not just entrepreneurship conferences; for example, Steve Blank and Alexander Osterwalder were among the key guests invited to the "Peter Drucker Forum" in November 2017 in Vienna. This suggests that Lean Startup is more likely to be a new school of management, and not a temporary fad.

Polish literature contains few attempts to explain and describe operations consistent with the Lean Startup methodology (Sońta-Drączkowska 2016; Popowska and Nalepa 2015; Ziębicki 2014). Most of these publications focus on business modelling as an interesting tool for business planning (Bis 2013; Drzewiecki 2013, 2016), but it is not presented as part of a larger, groundbreaking concept of organisation management (see Drzewiecki 2016; Białek-Jaworska et al. 2015). A similar reluctance can be noticed in foreign literature, especially among European researchers, whom one can sense distancing themselves from American pragmatism and tools that utilise "yellow post-it notes". It can even be said that the concept is often treated with disdain by science, because it does not have sufficient grounding in the theory of economics—which, as is clear from the literature discussed earlier, is not entirely true (cf. Teece 2010; Frederiksen and Brem 2017). It can also be assumed that the reason for Lean Startup and the startups themselves not being treated seriously by economists is a neoclassical "gigantomania", which implies that only the largest players exert real influence on the economy: governments, large companies, global corporations, with the size here measured by the number of employees, branches, and the capitalisation of assets. Startups do not fit this vision because they usually employ few people, do not multiply offices, and the resources they have are mostly immaterial.

This situation again refers to the issue of the disconnect between theory and management practice: academics were not able to predict, explain, or solve the problem of the lack of effective strategies, methods, and tools for startup management, which led to the spectacular bursting of the so-called dotcom bubble at the turn of the twentieth century. And thus entrepreneurs themselves have created effective tools and developed a functional model, which science dismisses with meaningful silence or diminishes its significance as insufficiently "scientific". This situation could, however, be treated quite differently, as an opportunity for revitalising the collaboration between science and business. Incomplete methodological foundations are a real weakness of Lean Startup and developing a stronger theoretical basis for this concept would undoubtedly work for the benefit of all stakeholders: entrepreneurs who use it and scientists who would have the opportunity to work with live, applicable models evolving and growing now. This is a promising direction for research efforts in the coming years, especially in view of the growing interest in Lean Startup from international corporations and many national governments.

3.5 Management Education

In management science, education has been for decades seen as a search for a happy medium between teaching the theory and educating for practice. In literature, this is known as the "rigour-relevance debate", where the question is asked about how research and teaching in management science can be rigorous—that is, correct in the sense of the applied scientific methodology—and at the same time useful for practitioners (Latusek-Jurczak and Prystupa-Rządca 2015; Czakon 2014).

Currently, the subjects of lively discussion include issues such as questioning the theory of economics as the foundation of management (cf. Khurana and Penrice 2011; Wang et al. 2011; Ferraro et al. 2005; Ghoshal 2005), neglect of ethical education (Andersson et al. 2007), critical thinking (Atwater et al. 2008), diversity (Bell et al. 2009), and the development of interpersonal skills (Ferraro et al. 2005). Question are also being asked on whether business education does not depart too far from the rigours of scientific discipline, losing a broader, strategic view of the problems under consideration and the ability to engage in a deep, holistic reflection (Hägg and Kurczewska 2016).

Following this train of thought, Andrzej Koźmiński (2011), citing the results of the Ford and Carnegie foundation reports from over half a century ago, wrote about the need for another "revolution" in the field of management education. He justified this need with fundamental changes:

- democratisation of the profession of manager, until recently identified with corporate business, and today also associated with such professions as doctor, farmer, chef, scientist;

- significant fragmentation of markets and, consequently, the development of numerous narrow management specialisations such as sports management, entertainment management, tourism management;
- globalisation of management education, which at the same time is characterised by a huge variation in the cost of access to it in the most developed countries (the United States and Western Europe), compared to other countries.

Koźmiński noted that "entrepreneurship" is currently still seen in schools as concerning small-scale manufacturing and uncomplicated family business (i.e. the so-called small business, discussed in Chap. 1), which noticeably eliminates elements of creative and unconventional (out of the box) thinking from the curricula. Meanwhile, what should be taught using the learning by doing method is, according to Koźmiński, precisely creative intellectual entrepreneurship and internal corporate entrepreneurship (intrapreneurship).

In the review paper devoted to research on management and business education, its authors, Ben Arbaugh et al. (2014), compiled the most cited works in the field of management and business education between 1970 and 2013. The authors searched for papers via Google Scholar using a broad definition of management education and searching for keywords in disciplines practised in business schools and discussed in scientific journals concerned with education. On this basis, they obtained 100 most cited works in 21 research categories. Two categories definitely dominated: entrepreneurship education (23 articles) and online education (22 articles). The next area, ethics for business students, had 12 articles on the list, and business school critiques ranked 4th with 9 articles, with the 3 most cited articles referring to this topic. Among the 25 items with over 300 citations, 8, or 1 in 3, covered entrepreneurship education.

Taking into account the last 20 years, 2 significant waves of publications on entrepreneurship education emerged: the first in 2000 (Cope and Watts 2000; Rae 2000; Rae and Carswell 2001), and the second after a special issue of the *Entrepreneurship: Theory and Practice* journal devoted entirely to the subject matter was published in 2005 (Cope 2005; Corbett 2005; Politis 2005). Gustaw Hägg and Agnieszka Kurczewska (2016) analysed these publications and ones that followed them, and concluded that the scientific output in the area of entrepreneurship education focused mainly on the process of transforming management practice into knowledge and on the importance of professional experiences as critical learning factors, with much less emphasis on understanding the experience itself as a source of knowledge. The authors posed a bold statement that entrepreneurship education is too limited, merely observing behaviours and entrepreneurship activities, and neglecting a deeper reflection on what is observed. This situation creates barriers to developing valuable knowledge in this area of science.

Among the latest directions of development in research on management education, two trends are currently noticeable (cf. *The Oxford Handbook of Management* 2017). The first one concerns the extent to which management education can occur in various, non-obvious and informal contexts—outside the school or university. This thinking is based in the thesis proposing a strong positive correlation between student engagement and effective learning. Daniel Feldman (2012, p. 263) described students' engagement as "the amount of time, energy and enthusiasm that students devote to acquiring new knowledge and skills, participating in extra-curricular vocational training and independently seeking work". In his work, the author suggests that, contrary to popular opinion and feeling, providing students with too many choices for professional development may in effect reduce their level of engagement in the activities they undertake.

The second trend in the development of education is problem-based learning. Although its effectiveness has already been demonstrated (Dochy et al. 2003), the current idea is to face the students with real business inquiries, which aims to develop skills complementary to knowledge, especially effective teamwork. As noted by Sandra Waddock and Josep Lozano (2013), holistic development of students requires the use of creative teaching methods. These authors analysed examples of classes that used problems to stimulate systemic thinking, reflection, and work in an interdependent and globalised world.[4] Then they turned their attention to a rarely discussed problem: in their opinion, research is needed not only on how to prepare students for new professional experiences, but also on the proper education of educators conducting these new kinds of classes. They require skills, the acquisition of which is time-consuming and difficult for

[4] In particular, they are studying a course in ESADE which combines single afternoon sessions, week-long sessions, and daily reflection in the form of a "journal", and a course at Boston College, titled *Leadership for Change* which combines full-day sessions, team learning, and individual reflection.

university-based educators, who are usually more focused on scientific activity than on teaching.

3.6 Education for Entrepreneurship

In the rich literature on entrepreneurship education, it is emphasised that it is a scientific field recognised by academicians (Kuratko 2005; Vesper and Gartner 1997), extremely important for the practitioners but not necessarily attractive for researchers planning academic careers (Kuckertz and Prochotta 2018; Kuckertz 2013). Numerous authors also state that it is a key element in building entrepreneurship economy and culture (McKeown et al. 2006; Matlay 2005; Kirby 2004; McMullan and Long 1987), also in Poland (Wach 2013). Most scholars agree that learning about entrepreneurship or some of its aspects is possible (Fayolle and Lassas-Clerc 2006; Henry et al. 2005a, b), and research by Alberta Charney and Gary Libecap (2000) proved that students educated in the direction of entrepreneurship were not only more inclined to set up their own businesses (which is a fairly obvious conclusion), but more often than others found employment in high-growing companies or were involved in important projects related to the development of new products within larger organisations.

The presence of entrepreneurship courses at universities is symbolically dated back to 1947, when they were launched at Harvard Business School. A few years later, in 1953, Peter Drucker led entrepreneurship and innovation classes at the University of New York. Francisco Liñán (2007) distinguished four categories of education for entrepreneurship:

- as a career path,
- in the area of launching companies,
- for mature entrepreneurs,
- promoting entrepreneurial attitudes: creativity, innovation, inventiveness, initiative.

Andreas Kuckertz (2011) additionally emphasises two elements that should be included in entrepreneurship curricula: providing entrepreneurship models with whom students could identify (case studies or meetings with entrepreneurs) and teaching using problem-based learning, learning by doing, and through internships in startups. Similarly, Krzysztof Wach (2013) points out that the entrepreneurship education curriculum should include such elements as developing entrepreneurial traits and skills as well as carrying out business projects.

Ernest Mwasalwiba (2010) is the author of a comprehensive, frequently cited review paper on entrepreneurship education, whose research goal was to determine the importance and general priorities of entrepreneurship education as well as the types of curricula, subject content, applied teaching methods, and indicators of the impact of this education. In his paper, Mwasalwiba drew attention to many key problems: the first of these was the ambiguity of the key definitions: entrepreneurship, enterprise, and entrepreneur (Cunningham and Lischeron 1991; Gartner 1990; Hébert and Link 1989), which raises further misunderstandings regarding the definition of entrepreneurship education itself (Pittaway and Cope 2007; Garavan and O'Cinneide 1994; Gartner 1990). Chaos in definitions and free-for-all interpretations have far-reaching implications for understanding goals of entrepreneurship education, defining specific course objectives, selecting target audiences, taught content, applied teaching methods, and ultimately assessing the results of teaching and its broadly understood effects (cf. Kurczewska 2013).

Another discussion concerns the goals of entrepreneurship education. Andreas Kuckertz (2011) asks about the goal of entrepreneurship education: is it the student becoming an entrepreneur at all, or being a "better" entrepreneur—if he or she becomes one? Significant in this discussion was the previously mentioned report by David Birch (1979, 1987), which, contrary to popular opinion at the time, showed that the main driving forces of the American economy were small businesses rather than large corporations. The importance of entrepreneurship is therefore greater than previously thought, and entrepreneurship education is more about developing awareness of the attractiveness of this career option than about specific changes in human behaviour. It is worth mentioning the concept of social entrepreneurship here, whose goal is to strengthen pro-social attitudes and support solutions to the most difficult problems of humanity (Yunus 2007). The need to take on *big ideas* appears very often in considerations related to the manifestations of entrepreneurship and entrepreneurship education, especially entrepreneurship based on knowledge and technological achievements (Byers et al. 2011). How to encourage entrepreneurs to take on difficult (and not trivial) challenges, and their investors to accept extraordinary risks?

According to Krzysztof Wach (2013), the aim of teaching entrepreneurship (in other words, education for entrepreneurship) is to promote creativity, innovation, and self-employment. This combination of educational goals was questioned by authors of a publication in which a clear distinction was made between entrepreneurship understood as self-employment and "Schumpeterian" entrepreneurship, that is, one generating a significant increase in wealth and employment. Magnus Henrekson and Tino Sanandaji (2014) argued that it is not about promoting self-employment as such, which does not contribute much to economic and social development, but rather supports the status quo. They argued that the experience of being educated for entrepreneurship has an unambiguously positive impact on the development of an entrepreneurial attitude in Schumpeter's sense—creative and innovative. This meant the creation and development of companies that are characterised by high growth rates and innovative implementations.

The latest works of Jerzy Cieślik (2014a, b, 2017) also address entrepreneurship education, listing harmful "illusions" in the perception of the phenomenon of entrepreneurship, for example, underestimating the role of product imitations and overestimating the importance of technological innovations. Duplication of this type of myths in the educational process may lead to repeating the same mistakes in the future and result in failed entrepreneurial attempts. In turn, Wach emphasises that in order to "achieve the desired effectiveness of education for entrepreneurship, there must occur a certain synergy of education programs (formal education) with informal forms of extracurricular or non-academic education. School and university education for entrepreneurship must therefore be supported by the institutional environment, in particular by broadly understood business practice" (Wach 2013, p. 251).

Mwasalwiba in the paper already discussed stated that entrepreneurship education is basically aimed at shaping or stimulating the attitude, spirit, and culture of entrepreneurship among people or in a community. The works he reviewed also included views that saw the creation of new companies and jobs as the goal of entrepreneurship education; others combined it with supporting communities by helping local entrepreneurs develop (Matlay 2005; Henry et al. 2005a, b; Kirby 2004; Vesper and Gartner 1997; McMullan and Long 1987). Finally, Mwasalwiba demonstrated that the impact of the educational programmes in question on entrepreneurship had not been clearly proven, mainly due to the lack of a generally accepted methodological framework for conducting such an assessment. Mwasalwiba's conclusions largely coincide with the conclusions of Pittway and Cope (2007), who found that entrepreneurship education certainly affects the willingness to undertake entrepreneurial initiatives, but it is not clear to what extent its graduates become better entrepreneurs.

Taking into account the discussed literature, one may wonder whether the main cause of the previous failures in studying the effects of entrepreneurship education does not lie in a general, excessively universal approach to this task. Since entrepreneurship is a broad concept and manifests itself in various ways, it might be easier to examine the impact of education on entrepreneurship using the division proposed by Henrekson and Sanandaji (2014), that is, to treat separately the effects such as self-employment and creation of small business and those related to undertaking creative, innovative, and dynamic initiatives in any form.

Another background to the debate on entrepreneurship education is the fact that higher education institutions are now facing an epochal challenge that involves their transformation into so-called entrepreneurship universities (Piotrowska-Piątek 2015; Czakon 2015; Urbaniec 2014; Wach 2014a; Gibb and Hannon 2006). Such a university (also called a "third generation university") opens itself to the needs of the socio-economic environment, in contrast to the classical Humboldt model, in which universities are autonomous "islands of knowledge" isolated from the environment (Piotrowska-Piątek 2015). A third generation university should combine intellectual capital with the needs of the market, and its mission, apart from scientific research and education, includes the promotion of entrepreneurship, innovation, and the stimulation of creativity. Such universities establish new types of relationships with the industry and state institutions, which benefit all parties to this so-called triple helix, bringing tangible benefits, including creation of clusters, that is, local, specialised, and highly competitive centres of industrial production, providing material for scientific research and education (Viale and Etzkowitz 2005). Henry Etzkowitz (2002) draws attention to a new model of academic career, where, next to the researcher "seeking the truth", there appears an "entrepreneurial academic" whose task is to transform knowledge into innovations useful for business. The attention of researchers, as well as more and more students, focuses on the commercial potential of acquired knowledge or research and experiments carried out. Laboratories that successfully complete projects for the industry (sometimes fulfilling their teaching mission at the same time) are a manifestation of the process of transforming many universities towards entrepreneurial science and teaching. Similarly, Kuckertz (2011) emphasised the need to understand

and implement the new "third mission" in universities (apart from research and teaching), which consists in adopting a broadly understood entrepreneurial culture. Jerzy Cieślik writes along similar lines, with suggestions based on experience from the implementation of educational programmes, including at Polish universities (Cieślik 2008; Cieślik et al. 2011).

Among Polish authors, there is general agreement that appropriate education at all levels is a critical condition for the development of entrepreneurship in Poland through shaping appropriate pro-entrepreneurship attitudes (see Rachwał and Wach 2016; Rachwał et al. 2016; Sułkowski 2016; Piróg 2015; Urbaniec 2014; Wach 2007, 2013, 2014b; Zioło 2013; Daszkiewicz 2013; Gaweł 2011; Pietrzykowski 2011; Cieślik 2006). As Małgorzata Kosała (2016) noticed, students on the one hand consider entrepreneurship as a subject definitely needed at universities and expect entrepreneurs to be included in the teaching process, but on the other hand present a relatively low level of engagement in this type of classes and activities that require their initiative, work, and time commitment.

A very interesting approach to this topic was adopted by the authors who analysed the "mythology of entrepreneurship", distinguishing as many as 58 myths divided into three categories: entrepreneur, entrepreneurial activity, entrepreneurial organisation (Bratnicki et al. 2002). These "myths" block entrepreneurial initiatives (selected myths are presented in Table 3.1). This paper inspired other authors who noticed that from this point of view, entrepreneurship education is nothing but the refutation of these myths in a creative, ingenious, and engaging way and "transforming views that block entrepreneurship into activities that stimulate entrepreneurship" (Noga and Noga 2016). The results of research conducted by Tomasz Rachwał and Krzysztof Wach additionally demonstrated that with the growth of positive individual attitudes towards entrepreneurial activity and entrepreneurs themselves, and with a greater sense of self-efficacy (agency), entrepreneurial intentions clearly increase among the surveyed students (Rachwał and Wach 2016).

In his subsequent publications, Krzysztof Wach has developed a consistent definitional framework and a transparent conceptual structure for entrepreneurship education. He proposes the adoption of a holistic understanding of the teaching process inspired by British guidelines in this regard.[5] These guidelines recommend combining actions to stimulate

[5] Quality Assurance Agency for Higher Education2012, *Enterprise and entrepreneurship education: guidance for UK higher education providers*, QAA, Gloucester, viewed 06 Nov 2017.

Table 3.1 Selected entrepreneurship "myths"

Scope	*Entrepreneurship myth*	*Scientific truth*
Entrepreneur	Entrepreneurs are born, so entrepreneurial behaviours cannot be learned	Everyone has the potential to become an entrepreneur by acquiring the right skills, knowledge, experience, and direct contacts
	An entrepreneur is distinguished by specific traits that form a typical profile	There is no standard entrepreneur profile. In fact, there are many types of entrepreneurs undertaking various ventures in multiple contexts. Motivation more than ability explains the attitude of an entrepreneur
	Entrepreneurs should be young, well-educated, and intelligent	Age is not a barrier to entrepreneurship. Entrepreneurial behaviours occur with different education. What is important are knowledge, experience, contacts, and professional training. The probability of success is increased by creativity, motivation, team building, leadership, analytical skills, and the ability to deal with ambiguity and adversity
Entrepreneurial activity	Starting a business is highly risky and often fails. The source of success is largely luck	Failures allow for learning through the acquisition of new experiences and are the engine of further entrepreneurial attempts. What seems to be "luck" is the result of knowledge and determination *Growing a business is much harder than starting it*
	If the entrepreneur has sufficient initial capital, they will not fail; money is the most important resource when starting a business	*Too much initial capital often leads to a lack of discipline, and consequently to impulsive spending* The money itself does not guarantee mobilising the appropriate, key resources for the venture
Entrepreneurial organisations	Small and medium-sized enterprises are the ones that create jobs	New jobs are created mainly by dynamically developing enterprises, regardless of their size
	Fast-growing organisations rely mainly on unique technology	*Fast-growing organisations rely mainly on people with high qualifications and competences*

Source: Own material based on: Bratnicki et al. (2002, pp. 3–6)

human creativity with the dissemination of general economic knowledge. Wach also proposes that the basic wording should have the form of "education for entrepreneurship", which occurs through formal or informal education, and which combines two aspects: entrepreneurial teaching and education in economics, including finance and business. Entrepreneurial teaching differs from ordinary teaching in that in addition to transferring knowledge and developing desired behaviours, it aims to "awaken" an entrepreneurial mindset, that is, to encourage a mental transformation, even personality transformation, with lasting consequences for the person's social activity. In turn, formal education for entrepreneurship comprises a minimum of three levels: elementary, secondary, and tertiary (Rachwał 2006), while informal education, apart from self-improvement and the acquisition of life experience, can take any form, including courses, workshops, training (also online, e.g. in the form of MOOC).

Wach (2014b) also proposed a conceptual diagram of education for entrepreneurship, consisting of three fundamental components:

1. economic (and financial) education—about the company's environment,
2. business education—about project management and operationalisation of activities,
3. individual (behavioural) education—about entrepreneurial dynamism, innovation, initiative, creativity, communication skills, and many other attitudes and skills that make up the broadly understood entrepreneurial, proactive attitude; it is the broadest component and the most difficult to develop.

Research conducted in the field of entrepreneurship education consists mainly in the preparation and implementation of teaching curricula, and then subjecting them to assessment and verification. Jeff Vanevenhoven (2013) wrote about the future of academic research in the field of education for entrepreneurship, which touched upon a fundamental problem, recurring in many studies: the insufficient proof of the impact of such education on economic practice. Vanevenhoven indicated the assessment of the effectiveness of various methods used in entrepreneurship education programmes as the main direction of research (cf. Skala 2016). He also discussed the ambiguous and often contradictory results of previous studies (cf. von Graevenitz et al. 2010; McNally et al. 2010; Souitaris et al. 2007; Weaver et al. 2006; Fayolle et al. 2006) and emphasised the importance of the publications which demonstrated better effectiveness of classes or courses meeting specific conditions. For example, training delivered by people who previously created startups themselves and curricula co-created by various representatives of the entrepreneurship ecosystem (e.g. investors, entrepreneurs, mentors) were shown to be more effective. Importantly, Vanevenhoven came to the simple conclusion that entrepreneurship education should (perhaps to a large extent) take place at an individual scale, since from a certain level of knowledge and skills, there is probably no universal optimal teaching process that can be implemented in any higher education institution. Vanevenhoven boldly claims that "we not only need to kick students out of the classroom, but we ourselves also need to get out of our offices and share these experiences directly with our students", which perfectly resonates with Steve Blank's suggestion for entrepreneurs using Lean Startup: "get out of the building, because you will not find answer to your business hypotheses there".

3.7 Education for Startups

If the economy, entrepreneurship, and education are coupled and feed back into each other (Ács et al. 2017; Ács and Audretsch 2010; Fayolle 2005; Honig 2004; Shepherd 2004; Block and Stumpf 1992; Birch 1987), correct "programming" of education can influence the shape of entrepreneurship and, consequently, of the entire economy—and vice versa. A significant role in this feedback is played by the entrepreneurship ecosystem, which has a positive and significant impact on the development of resource- and labour-productivity-based economies (although in the most innovative economies this relationship is much weaker). This means that in developing countries, a well-functioning entrepreneurship ecosystem can accelerate economic growth. The key factors determining the pace of this growth include, in addition to easily adopted technology, human capabilities and institutions that shape them (Ács et al. 2017).

The knowledge about the behaviour of modern organisations is then immediately incorporated in the curricula so as not to create (enlarge) the gap between knowledge and practical skills. This particularly applies to startup projects that function in an environment that changes so quickly that developing open and learning-focused attitudes among entrepreneurs is crucial (Cieślik and Skala 2016). In this context Agnieszka Kurczewska (2012) drew attention to effectuation (Sarasvathy 2008) as a universal and pragmatic logic of thinking, which is typically characteristic of entrepreneurs who create new products in new markets under conditions of significant uncertainty. Effectuation thinking works with non-linear management methodologies such as Lean Startup and facilitates their implementation, and also takes into account the importance of the network of contacts and belonging to the community—as the capital that entrepreneurs have at their disposal and in the function of which they develop their ventures. Effectuation helps to achieve success in the dynamically changing business environment, because the inability to effectively anticipate even the near future may be a critical mental barrier for many managers. At the same time, it is possible to learn effectuation, and it also often occurs spontaneously and unconsciously, in parallel with classic cause-and-effect thinking. And thus, if it's possible to learn effectuation, there is a chance for a breakthrough in developing pro-entrepreneurship attitudes within the educational process. As Kurczewska points out to business plans as a manifestation of cause-and-effect thinking, then a thesis can be proposed that business modelling as a key element of the Lean Startup management methodology is a manifestation of effectuation.

Literature review showed that entrepreneurship education applies to entrepreneurship in a broad sense, including self-employment and small business. It is therefore worth clearly distinguishing "education for startups" which focuses on innovative and dynamic forms of entrepreneurship, as well as specific industries associated with the commercial application of digital technologies.

Education for startups would thus mean educational programmes whose aim is to prepare students for the best "penetration" into the startup entrepreneurship ecosystem—consisting not only of entrepreneurs, but also of other participants, such as investment funds, state institutions, research and scientific units, media, community leaders, corporations, law firms, and many more. The modification of Wach's "education for entrepreneurship" model would thus consist in adapting the content of three teaching components to the specifics of startups (Fig. 3.3).

Education for startups, just like education for entrepreneurship, is based on three pillars. The first of these is economic education, which includes knowledge about the business environment and concerns mainly economics, entrepreneurship ecosystems, and new technologies and trends—which is especially important for startups. Business education is teaching about business management methods, in the case of startups, about Lean Startup, and especially about innovative business models. The

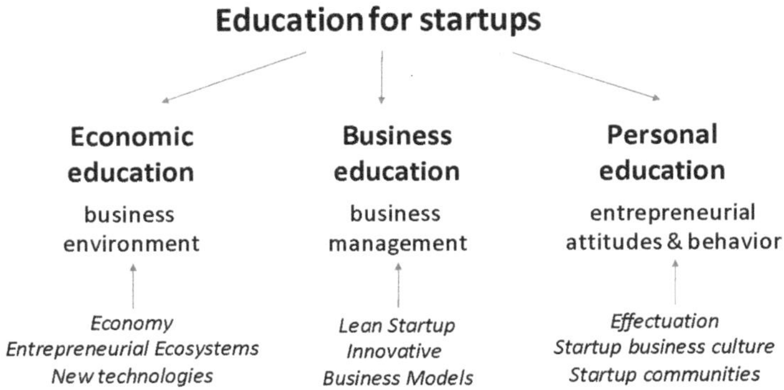

Fig. 3.3 Model of the education for startups. (Source: Own material based on: Wach 2014a)

third pillar is individual education, which refers to the soft aspects of the functioning of startups, that is, entrepreneurial attitudes and behaviours. It consists in instilling (or strengthening) effectuation and introducing students to startup business culture and startup communities. It can be argued that among the three listed elements of education for startups, the last one is of particular importance for increasing the probability of success, both for the venture and for its creators.

Education for Startups: Examples of Author's Own Implementations

Warsaw University of Technology: Innovative Entrepreneurship

The project named "Implementation of pilot educational programs in the field of Innovative Entrepreneurship at the Warsaw University of Technology" consisted in incorporating into the education system of the university teaching modules that develop pro-entrepreneurship professional orientation among the students.

The first classes in Innovative Entrepreneurship at the Warsaw University of Technology were launched at the Faculty of Transport in the winter semester of the academic year 2007/2008 as part of the WIPA (Educators of Academic Innovative Entrepreneurship) project.[6] It

[6]WIPA: The WIPA initiative has evolved over time into the SEIPA programme: Education Network of Academic Innovative Entrepreneurship, a project with a greater range and recognition in the community connected to entrepreneurship education at universities in Poland.

was an elective lecture (30 hours) for students of the last two years (of what was at the time a uniform Master's course) (2 points ECTS-European Credit Transfer System). The class turned out to be a success—in terms of both the number of interested students and the opinions they expressed about the high usefulness of the acquired knowledge and skills. These experiences prompted the idea of expanding Innovative Entrepreneurship teaching to other faculties of the University. Teaching in this area had taken place at the University, but it was scattered, as the teaching offer related to entrepreneurship was usually the result of individual initiatives undertaken by individual lecturers at their respective faculties. The idea met with the support of the University authorities, and acquired the support of the coordinator of the WIPA programme, Prof. Jerzy Cieślik.

The funds available under Sub-measure 4.1.1 Human Capital Operational Program (HC OP) were considered the best source of funding for the project, which ensured funding of projects in their entirety. The application for funding was submitted to the Ministry of Science and Higher Education in March 2009 and soon the project was qualified for funding.

The project "Implementation of pilot educational programs in the field of Innovative Entrepreneurship at the Warsaw University of Technology" can be considered a successful implementation with the use of EU funding. In the course of the project:

- a resource was created in the form of a team of qualified entrepreneurship lecturers (16 people), who at that time took part in leading conferences and training on entrepreneurship education (e.g. Aalto University, Cambridge University, Edinburgh University);
- in some cases, students actually founded companies and received mentoring support from the lecturers;
- more than 1200 students were trained at 16 faculties of the Warsaw University of Technology;
- the entrepreneurship education curriculum was improved on the basis of the experience and thanks to regularly (once a semester) organised seminars for lecturers.

The next step, which will complete the project in a certain way, will be to examine the development of careers of the graduates of the programme in terms of the impact of the entrepreneurship courses on their professional decisions.

Warsaw University of Technology: "Startup Management"[7]

During the implementation of the project of introducing entrepreneurship teaching programmes at the Warsaw University of Technology, the curriculum evolved. The changes were a result of the learning process and lecturers' improving qualifications. Each of the overlapping stages of professional development had its specificity and influenced the shape of the educational programmes implemented later. The first two projects—WIPA and SEIPA—were the time for acquiring qualifications as a lecturer of entrepreneurship, learning the classic teaching methods in this area, supported by a textbook (Cieślik 2006) and a website (www.seipa.edu.pl). The phase of implementation of the SEIPA-Warsaw University of Technology project was primarily concerned with organisational activity and acquiring knowledge about activities related to the development of entrepreneurship in the space of a university (cf. Cieślik et al. 2011). At the same time, a process of active penetration into the community of enterprises based on information processing technologies (ICT) took place, which involved learning about the mechanisms of their creation as well as the techniques and tools for managing such ventures. This activity was complemented by taking part in the first edition of training for entrepreneurship educators, organised by the National Collegiate Inventors and Innovators Alliance at the University of California, Berkeley.

Significant changes occurred within the teaching process:

- lectures were replaced with project-based learning incorporating elements of a lecture—a seminar;
- five-year business plans in spreadsheets gave way to business modelling based on the BMC (Osterwalder and Pigneur 2010[8]);
- an e-learning platform supporting interactive two-way communication replaced a web portal for one-way communication with students, acting as a repository of materials;

[7] More on this matter in Skala, A. (2015).

[8] The materials can be downloaded under a Creative Commons licence from the company website owned by Alexander Osterwalder: www.strategyzer.com

- in addition to the traditional teacher-students interaction model, some classes used the "flipped classroom" formula, where the students presented results of work they did between the classes (cf. Herreid and Schiller 2013; Enfield 2013). In this situation, the lecturer adopts the role of a student and comments, along with other participants, on the work done by the students;
- the key element of the classes is the confrontation of the project concept developed by the students with their potential clients using the "get out of the building" formula, through designing, conducting, and analysing interviews that test the business hypotheses developed at the stage of business modelling and/or working on the value proposition;
- the goal of the classes is to create prototypes of projects on which students work;
- instead of a traditional exam or coursework assessment, a public presentation of projects takes place, to which guests are invited, mainly entrepreneurs and investors, and their assessment influences the final subject grade.

Figure 3.4 presents the main elements forming the basic curriculum of the classes.

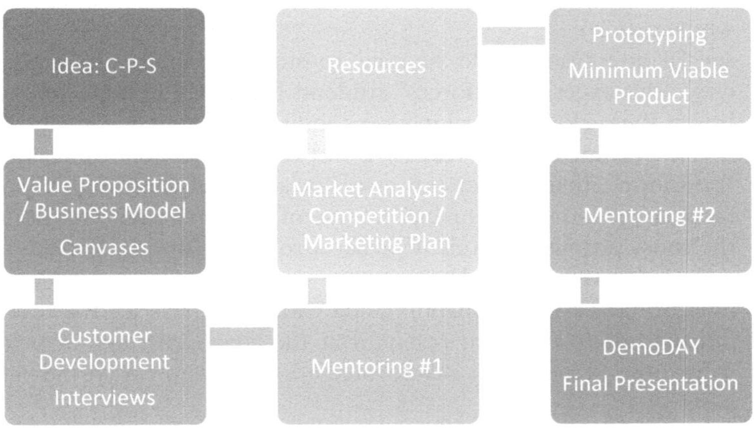

Fig. 3.4 The main elements of the curriculum of classes on startup management. (Source: Own material)

The most important challenges that the lecturer faces include (Skala 2015):

- in addition to the transfer of specific knowledge, it is important to point out sources of knowledge and the ways in which it can be acquired and updated independently;
- common myths and incorrect attitudes, for example, "I will not share my idea, because someone will steal it from me", "the first million must be stolen"; in practice, this means that discussions are going to take place during the classes, for which the lecturer must be prepared;
- it is important that the classes are not compulsory; obligatory participation is not conducive to good results;
- the course should have approximately 30 participants at any time, with 8 to 10 groups of 3 to 5 persons, preferably run in the interfaculty mode;
- it is worth highlighting the importance and value of business activity in the development of the economy, especially innovation- and knowledge-based activity;
- the value of the classes is significantly increased by the following factors: working with well-selected case studies, visits from entrepreneurs, evoking and controlled confrontation of different students' opinions, implementing prototypes (at least one per semester for the whole group);
- special attention should be paid to students' interviews with clients—this experience "forces" students from behind their desks and brings them closer to real market conditions;
- it is important that the teacher is not only a "lecturer", but also an "educator", that is, they possesses social capital (position and contacts in the entrepreneurship ecosystem), who can realistically help the most promising student projects to materialise in the business reality after the end of the course;
- mentoring is a very demanding and exhausting task for the teacher, but it leads to excellent results if at the advanced stage of project work time (15–30 min.) is devoted to each team on an individual basis.
- negative but credible verification of the business concept is assessed positively by the teacher as a result of the student's work;

- when educating students of technical sciences, one encounters their resistance, caused by their being used to unequivocal answers to the problems in the realm of hard sciences; in the case of testing business hypotheses, such answers often cannot be quickly and simply obtained and it is important to create a classroom atmosphere that will help the students to get used to this—psychologically difficult for them—situation.

The most difficult challenge of entrepreneurship education is, however, that the effects of this education can be seen, at the earliest, after a few or even more than ten years. It is also the reason for delayed possibility of verification of the effectiveness of implemented educational programmes. In the shorter term, only isolated cases of entrepreneurial attempts give the opportunity to observe and verify the taught knowledge and skills in practice.

SPIN Innovation Nest Entrepreneurship School: Workshops for Startups[9]

Innovation Nest Entrepreneurship School SPIN "is a model example of an academic spin-off company set up by an academic whose main goal was the commercialisation of knowledge" (Korpysa 2016, p. 217). The company was founded in 2011 and its activity focuses on education, which involves running business workshops (training) for startups functioning in the digital industry, including business model verification and business communication—in line with the assumptions of the Lean Startup methodology. The workshops are used by startups themselves, but it's the institutions that belong to the startup ecosystem that provide the funding: municipal authorities that care about the development of startup communities, technology parks, business centres, and so on.

The workshops utilise a proprietary education programme based on two elements: the Lean Startup methodology and Polish case studies developed as part of SPIN. The workshops focus on formulating hypotheses regarding, in the first place, the client-problem-solution triad (C-P-S), and then, the complete business model. Step by step, each hypothesis is tested in confrontation with the opinion and behaviour of potential customers thanks to the planned and completed interviews. The precise

[9] More on this subject in Cieślik and Skala (2016).

selection of respondents that entrepreneurs talk to and the correct preparation for asking questions are important. Some workshops end with the so-called Demo Day, a public event where startups present their projects to investors, business partners, or other stakeholders.

The starting point for creating the core of the training programme is the belief that correct business modelling and effective communication and presentation of a business venture have two main components. The first and the most important component is the correct preparation of the project itself. Such preparation requires the knowledge of the Lean Startup concept and the mastery of the toolkit used to implement it in the practice of managing a project. This primarily means business modelling based on the BMC, the ability to conduct customer development interviews, and building MVPs. The second component is acquiring competences related to the communication and presentation process itself, that is, the ability to develop the so-called pitch (or elevator pitch)—appropriate in terms of structure, content, and presentation method. Thus, these two elements—project testing and "pitch"—are at the core of every SPIN workshop.

The target group for the workshops consists of digital startups at various stages of development.

The result of the workshop is acceleration, that is, speeding up the growth of the best startups that take part in the workshops. In this context, it is worth noting that sometimes the teams interrupt their participation in the training programme in order to verify the fundamental assumptions of their projects as inspired by the training. Such situations are treated as educational successes, which prevent the wasting of valuable and rare resources available to startup founders and their potential investors. At the end of each workshop cycle, an assessment survey is carried out among the participants.

The training programme consists of the following elements:

- Recruitment stage: Teams are recruited online, according to a tried and tested formula. Various communication channels are used for this purpose, mainly social media portals. The application form allows for getting to know the projects better early in the application process, and the final selection of projects for the workshop is made by the SPIN team.
- Preparation for the workshops: MOOC online materials and reading case studies.

- Group workshops: Part 1 is devoted mostly to Lean Startup: theoretical introduction, case studies discussion, working with the tools, preparing for independent interview sessions.
- "Get out of the building" session: Independent work and individual consultations—each team has the right to two half-hour consultations with online tutors; during this session the teams carry out the customer discovery tasks themselves, which requires about ten hours of team work: conducting and processing the interviews and, if necessary, individual consultations with the tutor (e.g. via Skype).
- Group workshops: Part 2, dedicated primarily to communication and preparation of the presentation for investors, that is, the "pitch": theoretical introduction and workshops devoted to the preparation of business communications, simulation sessions using media recordings.
- Pitch Day event: project presentations by programme participants in a "Demo Day"/"Startup Weekend" formula. The audience consists of investors and entrepreneurs; after the presentation a question and answer session takes place.

During its operation, Innovation Nest Entrepreneurship School has carried out more than 40 educational workshops for startups, in which approximately 250 teams and almost 500 people have participated. This means that the people forming the SPIN team are among the best "networked" and, as a consequence, well-recognised figures in the Polish startup community. This wide network of contacts is a great asset in the operations, in which interpersonal relations are a fundamental component.

Contact is maintained with the workshops' "graduates"—in the context of building cooperation networks, supporting acceleration, and potentially investment. This is always highly appreciated in the assessment questionnaires completed by the participants of the workshops as an additional value of the educational programmes.

The workshop graduates include Timeself, Design4Europe, Webflow, Teleport.me, UniwersytetDzieci.pl, PocketPill, Privacy Protector, Sugentum, SquareIt!/Borrowl.com, Feeldate, Placechallenge, Icount, Flywithmonkey.com, ScatchApp, 4Decision, Quotiss, Mamapożycza, Jumbster, and many more. Some of them are still active (some under a different name), some have changed their form, and some have ceased to operate. SPIN Innovation Nest Entrepreneurship School has run workshops in collaboration with the following institutions in the Polish startup ecosystem: Warsaw Technological Space ("Smolna" Entrepreneurship Center, "Targowa" Creativity Center), Krakow Technology Park, Google Poland, Polish National Chamber of Commerce, Reaktor Warsaw.

3.8 Chapter Summary

This chapter has presented a methodology for managing a startup—Lean Startup—against the background of the history of the development of management science. Classic management schools have been presented and the characteristics of the art of management in Poland was developed, taking into account historical and social factors—especially in relation to the period in which Poland lacked statehood and the deep system transformation after 1989. The problematic attitude to entrepreneurs and entrepreneurship, which is the legacy of these periods, still affects entrepreneurial attitudes and business culture in Poland. Startups, as a new form of organisation, are a challenge for traditional methods and tools of venture management and create a climate for the development of entrepreneurship which is different from one that is rooted in Poland. The technocratic spirit originating from the large-scale manufacturing industry, the tradition of family businesses and crafts, and the experience of intuitive management in the times of systemic transformation clash with the startup culture which is open, social, and energetic, as well as nomadic and labile, and uses hermetic jargon. On the one hand, these attributes of startup culture are a source of its strength and potential, and, on the other hand, they can be a barrier for its rapid adoption and development in Poland.

Worldwide, the new management methodology exemplified by Lean Startup has so far been a subject of limited interest from the scientific community. The theoretical foundations of this method, which are insufficiently well grounded in science, are the source of disputes and discussions about the importance and durability of this direction in management, and the methods used in Lean Startup, considered to be not serious by many, sometimes invoke disrespectful attitudes. The lack of reliable data on the importance of startups for the economy and the recurring motif of waiting for or predicting another high-tech market bubble also contribute to those attitudes. It can be stated that the promising directions for further research include, on the one hand, developing a coherent and credible theoretical basis for a new startup management methodology and, on the other hand, creating a common methodological framework for identifying this market and metrics that will describe it, especially in terms of its importance for the broadly understood economy and social development.

Startups as a new, specific form of organisation operating within the framework of innovative, dynamic technological entrepreneurship are a challenge for education at all levels—including lifelong learning. This challenge concerns three main areas:

1. the definition of entrepreneurship and education for entrepreneurship, and the definition of a startup and education for startups;
2. new startup management methodologies and effective methods for teaching them;
3. methods and metrics used to assess the effectiveness of education, that is, its real impact on entrepreneurial attitudes and initiatives.

There is a rich, though immature, scientific output relating to education for entrepreneurship. Works on the structure and curriculum of classes as well as specific teaching techniques and methods dominate this output. There is a lack of review and strategic studies outlining the most important directions of research and discussing its application. Knowledge about education for entrepreneurship can be described as dispersed, and the immaturity of this subdiscipline is demonstrated by unresolved disputes and discussions about definitions and terminology. The authors dealing with this subject agree that education for entrepreneurship has a powerful impact on business and pro-entrepreneurship attitudes, but a satisfactory methodology has not yet been developed that would allow for an unambiguous proof of the existence and direction of this relationship. At the same time, education is not seen as a specialist research direction guaranteeing a fast academic career, and in any case there are other specialisations in the area of entrepreneurship science, which are perceived as more attractive in this respect. This threatens this speciality with being the subject of negative choices by young entrepreneurial researchers.

Within the three main components of education for startup entrepreneurship—economic, business, and individual education—the last one is growing in importance. It is mainly about stimulating effectuation thinking, instilling startup culture, and showing the benefits of creating and actively participating in startup communities. The hypothesis that non-formal education is used more often than formal channels in order to acquire individual education appears to be quite strong, which creates a serious challenge for the system of institutional education for startup entrepreneurship.

In relation to the structure of the classes themselves, on the one hand, the challenge is to ensure a high level of engagement from participating students, and, on the other hand, to anchor these classes within a university and local (e.g. city-wide) entrepreneurship ecosystem, which will provide the opportunity to incubate and accelerate the best projects and/or teams that emerge during classes.

Formal education for startups, understood as an institutional education system fostering initiatives aiming to create and develop startups, is currently one of the weakest, if not the weakest, links in the startup ecosystem in Poland. This thesis cannot be supported by the results of scientific research, because no such research has been carried out, but it results from long-term observation of this community, from participation in numerous debates on this issue, and, indirectly, from the results of the "Polish Startups" study.[10] This does not mean that there are no excellent initiatives in the field of education for entrepreneurship and for startups undertaken by many institutions—on the contrary, more and more such projects appear. However, the scope and intensity of these activities must be considered to be very inadequate.

References

Ács, Z. J., & Audretsch, D. B. (2010). Knowledge spillover entrepreneurship. In *Handbook of entrepreneurship research*. New York: Springer.

Ács Z. J., Estrin, S., Mickiewicz, T., & Szerb, L. (2017). *Institutions, entrepreneurship and growth: The role of national entrepreneurial ecosystems*. Available at SSRN: https://ssrn.com/abstract=2912453. Accessed 31 Jan 2018.

Adamczyk, M. (2016). Koncepcje zarządzania innowacjami na przykładzie krakowskich start-upów technologicznych. *Przegląd Organizacji, 7*, 41–45.

Andersson, L. M., Giacalone, R. A., & Jurkiewicz, C. L. (2007). On the relationship of hope and gratitude to corporate social responsibility. *Journal of Business Ethics, 70*(4), 401–409.

Andries, P., Debackere, K., & Looy, B. (2013). Simultaneous experimentation as a learning strategy: Business model development under uncertainty. *Strategic Entrepreneurship Journal, 7*(4), 288–310.

[10] The survey asked about the sources of knowledge that entrepreneurs use and the degree of their influence on the activities they undertake. Formal sources of knowledge and educational institutions were mentioned in the last places among the obtained answers (Beauchamp et al. 2017).

Arbaugh, J. B., Fornaciari, C., & Hwang, A. (2014). Development patterns in business and management education research: Knowledge-based or knower-based? *Academy of Management Proceedings, 2014*(1), 1232.

Atwater, J. B., Kannan, V. R., & Stephens, A. A. (2008). Cultivating systemic thinking in the next generation of business leaders. *Academy of Management Learning & Education, 7*(1), 9–25.

Backhaus, K. B., Stone, B. A., & Heiner, K. (2002). Exploring the relationship between corporate social performance and employer attractiveness. *Business & Society, 41*(3), 292–318.

Batra, R., Ahuvia, A., & Bagozzi, R. P. (2012). Brand love. *Journal of Marketing, 76*(2), 1–16.

Bauman, Z., & Kunz, T. (2006). *Płynna nowoczesność.* Kraków: Wydawnictwo Literackie.

Beauchamp, M., Kowalczyk, A., & Skala, A. (2017). *Polish startups. Report 2017.* Warsaw: Startup Poland.

Becker, A., Knyphausen-Aufseß, D. Z., & Brem, A. (2015). Beyond traditional developmental models: A fresh perspective on entrepreneurial new venture creation. *International Journal of Entrepreneurial Venturing, 7*(2), 152–172.

Bell, M. P., Connerley, M. L., & Cocchiara, F. K. (2009). The case for mandatory diversity education. *Academy of Management Learning & Education, 8*(4), 597–609.

Białek-Jaworska A., Gabryelczyk R., & Pugacewicz A. (2015). *Czy komercjalizacja wyników badań nauko- wych wpływa na dojrzałość modelu biznesowego?* Przedsiębiorczość i Zarządzanie, *16*(11), issue 2: *Zarządzanie – nowe perspektywy: heurystyczne podejście do innowacyjności.*

Birch, D. L. (1979). *The job generation process.* Cambridge, MA: MIT Program on Neighborhood and Regional Change.

Birch, D. L. (1987). *Job creation in America: How our smallest companies put the most people to work.* New York: The Free Press.

Bis, J. (2013). Innowacyjny model biznesowy – sposób na zwiększenie przewagi konkurencyjnej. *Przedsiębiorczość i Zarządzanie, 14*(13), issue 2: *Modele biznesowe,* 53–63.

Blank, S. (2003). *The four steps to the epiphany: Successful strategies for products that win.* Pescadero: K&S Ranch.

Blank, S. (2013). Why the lean start-up changes everything. *Harvard Business Review, 91*(5), 63–72.

Blank, S. (2016). Why visionary CEOs never have visionary successors. *Harvard Business Review.* http://hbr.org/2016/10/why-visionary-ceos-never-have-visionary-successors. Accessed 17 Jan 2017.

Blank, S., & Dorf, B. (2012). *Startup owner's manual.* Pescadero: K&S Ranch Inc.

Błaszczak, A., & Ogonowska-Rejer, A. (2016). Przynajmniej dwóch na pięciu szefów czołowych przedsię- biorstw to absolwenci uczelni technicznych. *Rzeczpospolita*. online. http://www.rp.pl/Sciezki%2D%2Dkariery/312069882-Najwiekszymi- rmami-w-Polsce-najczesciej-zarzadzaja-inzynierowie.html. Accessed 6 Dec 2016.

Block, Z., & Stumpf, S. A. (1992). Entrepreneurship education research: Experience and challenge. In D. L. Sexton & J. D. Kasarda (Eds.), *The state of the art of entrepreneurship*. Boston: PWS-Kent Publishing.

Bratnicki, M., Dyduch, W., & Gabryś, B. J. (2002). Mity przedsiębiorczości w polskich organizacjach: diagnoza i mechanizmy ożywiania potencjału przedsiębiorczości. In P. Wachowiak, M. Dąbrowski, & B. Majewski (Eds.), *Kształtowanie postaw przedsiębiorczych a edukacja ekonomiczna*, materiały konferencyjne. Warszawa.

Byers, T. H., Dorf, R. C., & Nelson, A. J. (2011). *Technology ventures: From idea to enterprise* (Vol. 3). New York: McGraw-Hill.

Castells, M., & Marody, M. (2013). *Społeczeństwo sieci*. Warszawa: WN PWN.

Charney, A., & Libecap, G. D. (2000). *The impact of entrepreneurship education: An evaluation of the Berger Entrepreneurship Program at the University of Arizona, 1985–1999*. Final report. https://ebr.eller.arizona.edu/sites/ebr/les/docs/research-studies/impact-of-entrepreneurship-education-1985-1999.pdf. Accessed 9 May 2018.

Chesbrough, H. (2006). *Open innovation: The new imperative for creating and profiting from technology*. Boston: Harvard Business Press.

Chesbrough, H. (2010). Business model innovation: Opportunities and barriers. *Long Range Planning, 43*(2), 354–363.

Christensen, C., & Raynor, M. (2013). *The innovator's solution: Creating and sustaining successful growth*. Boston: Harvard Business Review Press.

Chrostowski, A., & Jemielniak, D. (2008). Action Research w teorii organizacji i zarządzania. *Organizacja i Kierowanie, 1*, 41–56.

Cieślik, J. (2006). *Przedsiębiorczość dla ambitnych: jak uruchomić własny biznes*. Warszawa: Wydawnictwa Akademickie i Profesjonalne.

Cieślik, J. (2008). *Kształcenie w zakresie przedsiębiorczości na poziomie akademickim*. http://www.fun-dacja.edu.pl/przedsiebiorczosc/_referaty/sesja_IIa/5.pdf. Accessed 30 Jan 2018.

Cieślik, J. (2014a). *Przedsiębiorczość, polityka, rozwój*. Warszawa: Wydawnictwo Akademickie Sedno.

Cieślik, J. (2014b). Iluzje innowacyjnej przedsiębiorczości. *Kwartalnik Nauk o Przedsiębiorstwie, 3*, 4–16.

Cieślik, J. (2015). Miejsce przedsiębiorczości w strukturze nauk o zarządzaniu. *Kwartalnik nauk o przedsiębiorstwie, 2*, 59–69.

Cieślik, J. (2017). *Entrepreneurship in emerging economies: Enhancing its contribution to socio-economic development*. Cham: Palgrave Macmillan.

Cieślik, J., & Skala, A. (2016). Nowe tendencje w kształceniu innowacyjnych przedsiębiorców. *Horyzonty Wychowania, 15*(34), 309–322.
Cieślik, J., Matusiak, K. B., Guliński, J., & Skala-Poźniak, A. (2011). *Edukacja dla przedsiębiorczości akademickiej.* Warszawa: Polska Agencja Rozwoju Przedsiębiorczości.
Clegg, S., Berti, S., & Jarvis, W. P. (2017). Future in the past: A philosophical reflection on the prospects of management. In A. Wilkinson, S. J. Armstrong, & M. Lounsbury (Eds.), *The Oxford handbook of management.* Oxford: Oxford University Press.
Collis, D. (2016). Lean strategy. *Harvard Business Review, 3,* 62–68.
Cooper, B., & Vlaskovits, P. (2010). *The entrepreneur's guide to customer development.* Norwich: Bertrams.
Cope, J. (2005). Toward a dynamic learning perspective of entrepreneurship. *Entrepreneurship Theory and Practice, 29*(4), 373–397.
Cope, J., & Watts, G. (2000). Learning by doing – An exploration of experience, critical incidents and reflection in entrepreneurial learning. *International Journal of Entrepreneurial Behaviour & Research, 6*(3), 104–124.
Corbett, A. C. (2005). Experiential learning within the process of opportunity identification and exploitation. *Entrepreneurship Theory and Practice, 29*(4), 473–491.
Cunningham, J. B., & Lischeron, J. (1991). Defining entrepreneurship. *Journal of Small Business Management, 29*(1), 45.
Czakon, W. (2014). Kryteria oceny rygoru metodologicznego badań w naukach o zarządzaniu. *Organization and Management, 1*(161), 51–62.
Czakon, W. (2015). Od humanizmu do kariery. Zmiany uniwersytetu dziś i jutro. In K. Jędralska & J. Bernais (Eds.), *Uniwersytet w perspektywie kształcenia przez całe życie* (pp. 103–112). Katowice: Wydawnictwo Uniwersytetu Ekonomicznego.
Czech, A. (2004). *Adamiecki, Hauswald, Rothert: w 100-lecie nauki organizacji i zarządzania w Polsce.* Katowice: Prace Naukowe/Akademia Ekonomiczna w Katowicach.
Daszkiewicz, N. (2013). Education as a stimulating factor for entrepreneurship development. *Horyzonty Wychowania, 13*(26), 165–177.
David, F. R., David, M. E., & David, F. R. (2011). What are business schools doing for business today? *Business Horizons, 54*(1), 51–62.
Dhaliwal, D. S., Li, O. Z., Tsang, A., & Yang, Y. G. (2011). Voluntary nonfinancial disclosure and the cost of equity capital: The initiation of corporate social responsibility reporting. *The Accounting Review, 86*(1), 59–100.
Dochy, F., Segers, M., van den Bossche, P., & Gijbels, D. (2003). Effects of problem-based learning: A meta-analysis. *Learning and Instruction, 13,* 533–568.

Drzewiecki, J. (2013). Model biznesu jako narzędzie zarządzania strategicznego: zastosowanie, dylematy i wyzwania. *Przedsiębiorczość i Zarządzanie, 14*(13), issue 2: *Modele biznesowe*, 65–75.
Drzewiecki, J. (2016). Zmienność modelu biznesowego w kontekście innowacyjności organizacji. *Management Forum, 1*(4), 11–16.
Enfield, J. (2013). Looking at the impact of the flipped classroom model of instruction on undergraduate multimedia students at CSUN. *TechTrends, 57*(6), 14–27.
Etzkowitz, H. (2002). Networks of innovation: Science, technology and development in the triple helix era. *International Journal of Technology Management & Sustainable Development, 1*(1), 7–20.
Fayolle, A. (2005). Evaluation of entrepreneurship education: Behavior performing or intention increasing? *International Journal of Entrepreneurship and Small Business, 2*(1), 89–98.
Fayolle, A., & Lassas-Clerc, N. (2006). Essay on the nature of entrepreneurship education. In *International Conference Entrepreneurship in United Europe-Challenges and Opportunities*.
Fayolle, A., Gailly, B., & Lassas-Clerc, N. (2006). Assessing the impact of entrepreneurship education programs: A new methodology. *Journal of European Industrial Training, 30*(9), 701–720.
Feld, B. (2012). *Startup communities: Building an entrepreneurial ecosystem in your city*. Hoboken: John Wiley & Sons.
Feldman, D. C. (2012). Student engagement: Selection, management, and outcomes. In B. Holtom & E. Dierdor (Eds.), *Disrupt or be disrupted: A blueprint for change in management education*. San Francisco: Jossey-Bass.
Ferraro, F., Pfeffer, J., & Sutton, R. I. (2005). Economics language and assumptions: How theories can become self-fulfilling. *Academy of Management Review, 30*(1), 8–24.
Frederiksen, D. L., & Brem, A. (2017). How do entrepreneurs think they create value? A scientific reflection of Eric Ries' Lean Startup approach. *International Entrepreneurship and Management Journal, 13*(1), 169–189.
Furr, N., & Ahlstrom, P. (2011). *Nail it then scale it: The entrepreneur's guide to creating and managing breakthrough innovation*. Lexington: NISI Institute.
Garavan, T. N., & O'Cinneide, B. (1994). Entrepreneurship education and training programmes: A review and evaluation – Part 1. *Journal of European Industrial Training, 18*(8), 3–12.
Gartner, W. B. (1990). What are we talking about when we talk about entrepreneurship? *Journal of Business Venturing, 5*(1), 15–28.
Gassmann, O., Sandmeier, P., & Wecht, C. (2006). Extreme customer innovation in the front-end: Learning from a new software paradigm. *International Journal of Technology Management, 33*(1), 46–65.
Gaweł, A. (2011). Kształcenie uniwersyteckie jako czynnik wpływający na przedsiębiorczość. *Zeszyty Naukowe Uniwersytetu Ekonomicznego w Poznaniu, 215*, 71–87.

Ghoshal, S. (2005). Bad management theories are destroying good management practices. *Academy of Management Learning & Education, 4*(1), 75–91.

Gibb, A., & Hannon, P. (2006). Towards the entrepreneurial university. *International Journal of Entrepreneurship Education, 4*(1), 73–110.

Glinka, B. (2008). *Kulturowe uwarunkowania przedsiębiorczości*. Warszawa: PWE.

Glinka, B., & Kostera, M. (red.). (2012). *Nowe kierunki w organizacji i zarządzaniu*. Warszawa: Wolters Kluwer.

Govindarajan, V., & Ramamurti, R. (2011). Reverse innovation, emerging markets, and global strategy. *Global Strategy Journal, 1*(3–4), 191–205.

Hägg, G., & Kurczewska, A. (2016). Connecting the dots: A discussion on key concepts in contemporary entrepreneurship education. *Education + Training, 58*(7/8), 700–714.

Hauser, J., Tellis, G., & Griffn, A. (2006). Research on innovation: A review and agenda for 'marketing science'. *Marketing Science, 25*(6), 687–717.

Hébert, R. F., & Link, A. N. (1989). In search of the meaning of entrepreneurship. *Small Business Economics, 1*(1), 39–49.

Henrekson, M., & Sanandaji, T. (2014). Small business activity does not measure entrepreneurship. *Proceedings of the National Academy of Sciences, 111*(5), 1760–1765.

Henry, C., Hill, F., & Leitch, C. (2005a). Entrepreneurship education and training: Can entrepreneurship be taught? Part I. *Education + Training, 47*(2), 98–111.

Henry, C., Hill, F., & Leitch, C. (2005b). Entrepreneurship education and training: Can entrepreneurship be taught? Part II. *Education + Training, 47*(3), 158–169.

Herreid, C. F., & Schiller, N. A. (2013). Case studies and the flipped classroom. *Journal of College Science Teaching, 42*(5), 62–66.

Hlupic, V. (2014). *The management shift: How to harness the power of people and transform your organization for sustainable success*. London: Palgrave Macmillan/Springer.

Hlupic, V. (2017). The frogs in hot water. *Dialog Review*. http://dialoguereview.com/frogs-hot-water/. Accessed 30 Oct 2017.

Honig, B. (2004). Entrepreneurship education: Toward a model of contingency-based business planning. *Academy of Management Learning & Education, 3*(3), 258–273.

Johnson, M. W., Christensen, C. M., & Kagermann, H. (2008). Reinventing your business model. *Harvard Business Review, 86*(12), 50–59.

Khurana, R., & Penrice, D. (2011). Business education: The American trajectory. In M. Morsing & A. S. Rovira (Eds.), *Business schools and their contribution to society*. London: Sage.

Kirby, D. A. (2004). Entrepreneurship education: Can business schools meet the challenge? *Education + Training, 46*(8/9), 510–519.

Korpysa, J. (2016). *Przedsiębiorczość jako proces tworzenia i funkcjonowania akademickich mikroprzedsiębiorstw spin-o w Polsce*. Szczecin: Wydawnictwo Naukowe Uniwersytetu Szczecińskiego.

Kosała, M. (2016). Edukacja przedsiębiorczości – analiza tendencji, metod i narzędzi w zakresie nauczania przedsiębiorczości w środowisku akademickim. *Horyzonty Wychowania, 15*(34), 49–66.

Koźmiński, A. K. (2011). The new revolution in management education? *Master of Business Administration, 19*(4), 2–6.

Koźmiński, A. K. (2014). Wkład zarządzania we wzrost gospodarczy. In G. W. Kołodko (Ed.), *Zarządzanie i polityka gospodarcza dla rozwoju*. Warszawa: Poltext.

Kuckertz, A. (2011). Entrepreneurship education – Status quo and prospective developments. *Journal of Entrepreneurship Education, 16*, 59–71.

Kuckertz, A. (2013). *What's hot in entrepreneurship research in 2013?* (The 1st of a series of annual trend surveys). Hohenheim: Universität Hohenheim.

Kuckertz, A., & Prochotta, A. (2018). *What's hot in entrepreneurship research in 2018?* (Hohenheim entrepreneurship research brief). Hohenheim: Universität Hohenheim.

Kuratko, D. F. (2005). The emergence of entrepreneurship education: Development, trends, and challenges. *Entrepreneurship Theory and Practice, 29*(5), 577–598.

Kurczewska, A. (2012). W jaki sposób myślą przedsiębiorcy? – czyli: „jeśli mogę kontrolować przyszłość, nie muszę jej przewidywać". *E-mentor, 5*(47). http://www.e-mentor.edu.pl/artykul/index/numer/47/id/965. Accessed 30 Oct 2017.

Kurczewska, A. (2013). *Przedsiębiorczość jako proces współoddziaływania sposobności i intencji przedsiębiorczych*. Warszawa: PWE.

Łada, M. (2016). Big Data wyzwaniem dla zarządzania i rachunkowości. *Studia Ekonomiczne, 299*, 197–206.

Ladd, T. (2016, March). The limits of the lean startup method. *Harvard Business Review*.

Ladd, T., Lyytinen, K., & Gemmell, R. (2015). How customer interaction and experimentation advance new venture concepts in a cleantech accelerator. *Academy of Management Proceedings, 2015*(1), 11415.

Lago, M. D., Corti, D., & Pedrazzoli, P. (2016). Turning a lean business model into a successful Start-up in the wearable technology sector: The case of Clara Swiss Tech. In R. Rinaldi & R. Bandinelli (Eds.), *Business models and ICT technologies for the fashion supply chain* (pp. 111–122). Cham: Springer International Publishing AG.

Lange, J. E., Mollov, A., Pearlmutter, M., Singh, S., & Bygrave, W. D. (2007). Pre-start-up formal business plans and post-start-up performance: A study of 116 new ventures. *Venture Capital, 9*(4), 237–256.

Latusek-Jurczak, D., & Prystupa-Rządca, K. (2015). Wykorzystanie profesjonalnych studiów przypadków w dydaktyce zarządzania. *Organizacja i Kierowanie, 4*, 191–203.

Liñán, F. (2007). The role of entrepreneurship education in the entrepreneurial process. In A. Fayolle (Ed.), *Handbook of research in entrepreneurship education* (pp. 230–247). Cheltenham/Northampton: Edward Elgar.

Matlay, H. (2005). Entrepreneurship education in UK business schools: Conceptual, contextual and policy considerations. *Journal of Small Business and Enterprise Development, 12*(4), 627–643.

Maurya, A. (2012). *Running lean: Iterate from plan A to a plan that works.* Sebastopol: O'Reilly Media.

McGrath, R. G. (2013). *The end of competitive advantage: How to keep your strategy moving as fast as your business.* Boston: Harvard Business Review Press.

McGrath, R. G., & MacMillan, I. C. (1995). *Discovery driven planning, Wharton School.* Philadelphia: Snider Entrepreneurial Center.

McGrath, R. G., & MacMillan, I. C. (2009). *Discovery-driven growth: A breakthrough process to reduce risk and seize opportunity.* Boston: Harvard Business Review Press.

McKeown, J., Millman, C., Reddy, S. S., Smith, K., & Martin, L. M. (2006). Graduate entrepreneurship education in the United Kingdom. *Education + Training, 48*(8/9), 597–613.

McMullan, W. E., & Long, W. A. (1987). Entrepreneurship education in the nineties. *Journal of Business Venturing, 2*(3), 261–275.

McNally, J. J., Martin, B. C., & Kay, M. J. (2010). *Examining the formation of human capital in entrepreneurship: A meta-analysis of entrepreneurship education outcomes.* Paper presented at the annual meeting of the academy of management, Montreal.

Mwasalwiba, E. S. (2010). Entrepreneurship education: A review of its objectives, teaching methods, and impact indicators. *Education + Training, 52*(1), 20–47.

Nicholas, J., Ledwith, A., & Perks, H. (2011). New product development best practice in SME and large organisations: Theory vs practice. *European Journal of Innovation Management, 14*(2), 227–251.

Noga, B., & Noga, M. (2016). Edukacja ekonomiczna społeczeństwa a edukacja przedsiębiorczości. *Studia i Prace WNEiZ US, 44*(2), 255–266.

Osterwalder, A. (2004). *The business model ontology: A proposition in a design science approach* (PhD thesis). Université de Lausanne, Ecole des Hautes Etudes Commerciales. http://www.acade-mia.edu/download/30373644/thebusiness-model-ontology.pdf. Accessed 30 Apr 2018.

Osterwalder, A., & Pigneur, Y. (2010). *Business model generation: A handbook for visionaries, game changers, and challengers.* Hoboken: John Wiley & Sons.

Owens, T., & Fernandez, O. (2014). *The lean enterprise: How corporations can innovate like startups.* Hoboken: John Wiley & Sons.

Picken, J. C. (2017a). From founder to CEO: The entrepreneur's roadmap. *Business Horizons, 60*(1), 7–14.
Picken, J. C. (2017b). From startup to scalable enterprise: Laying the foundation. *Business Horizons, 60*(5), 587–595.
Pietrzykowski, M. (2011). Entrepreneurship in higher education – The case of Poland. In M. Dabić & M. Pietrzykowski (Eds.), *Fostering education in entrepreneurship*. Poznań: Wydawnictwo Naukowe Bo- gucki.
Piketty, T. (2014). *Capital in the twenty-first century*. Cambridge, MA: Harvard University Press.
Piotrowska-Piątek, A. (2015). O trzeciej misji szkół wyższych w Polsce w świetle analizy ich misji i strategii rozwoju. *Organizacja i Kierowanie, 3*, 151–165.
Piróg, D. (2015). Kompetencje z zakresu przedsiębiorczości: rozważania teoretyczne i ich ilustracje w ob- szarze szkolnictwa wyższego. *Przedsiębiorczość-Edukacja, 11*, 364–376.
Pittaway, L., & Cope, J. (2007). Entrepreneurship education: A systematic review of the evidence. *International Small Business Journal, 25*(5), 479–510.
Politis, D. (2005). The process of entrepreneurial learning: A conceptual framework. *Entrepreneurship Theory and Practice, 29*(4), 399–424.
Popowska, M., & Nalepa, P. (2015). Lean Startup as a new way of managing technology ventures illustrated by the example of Wilcome App, Wydział Zarządzania Uniwersytetu Warszawskiego. *Studia i Materiały, 2*(19), 7–21.
Power, B. (2014, April). How GE applies lean startup practices. *Harvard Business Review*.
PricewaterhouseCoopers. (2014). *17th annual global CEO survey: Fit for the future*. https://www.pwc.com/ve/en/publicaciones/encuesta-global-anual-de-ceo.html. Accessed 20 Feb 2017.
Rachwał, T. (2006). Kształtowanie postaw przedsiębiorczych w edukacji szkolnej. In B. Muchacka (Ed.), *Szkoła w nauce i praktyce edukacyjnej* (Vol. 2). Kraków: Oficyna Wydawnicza Impuls.
Rachwał, T., & Wach, K. (2016). Badanie intencji przedsiębiorczych młodego pokolenia: wyniki ankietyzacji wśród studentów kierunków nieekonomicznych. *Przedsiębiorczość-Edukacja, 12*, 405–415.
Rachwał, T., Kurek, S., & Boguś, M. (2016). Entrepreneurship education at secondary level in transition economies: A case of Poland. *Entrepreneurial Business and Economics Review, 4*(1), 61–81.
Rae, D. (2000). Understanding entrepreneurial learning: A question of how? *International Journal of Entrepreneurial Behaviour and Research, 6*(3), 145–159.
Rae, D., & Carswell, M. (2001). Towards a conceptual understanding of entrepreneurial learning. *Journal of Small Business and Enterprise Development, 8*(2), 150–158.

Reiser, D. B. (2011). Benefit corporations—A sustainable form of organization. *Wake Forest Law Review, 46*, 591.

Ries, E. (2011). *The lean startup: How today's entrepreneurs use continuous innovation to create radically successful businesses.* New York: Crown Business.

Royce, W. W. (1987). Managing the development of large software systems: Concepts and techniques. In W. E. Riddle (Ed.), *Proceedings of the 9th International Conference on Software Engineering* (pp. 328–338). Monterey: IEEE Computer Society Press.

Salerno, M. S., de Vasconcelos Gomes, L. A., da Silva, D. O., Bagno, R. B., & Freitas, S. L. T. U. (2015). Innovation processes: Which process for which project? *Technovation, 35*, 59–70.

Sarasvathy, S. (2001). Causation and effectuation: Toward a theoretical shift from economic inevitability to entrepreneurial contingency. *Academy of Management Review, 26*(2), 243–263.

Sarasvathy, S. (2008). *Effectuation: Elements of entrepreneurial expertise.* Northampton: Edward Elgar Publishing.

Shane, S. A., & Venkataraman, S. (2000). The promise of entrepreneurship as a field of research. *Academy of Management Review, 25*, 217–226.

Shepherd, D. A. (2004). Educating entrepreneurship students about emotion and learning from failure. *Academy of Management Learning & Education, 3*(3), 274–287.

Skala, A. (2015). Przedsiębiorczość-wyzwanie dla edukacji. In A. Pustuła, J. Majczyk, & M. Darecki (Eds.), *Przedsiębiorczość: jednostka, organizacja, kontekst.* Warszawa: Wydawnictwo Naukowe Wydziału Zarządzania Uniwersytetu Warszawskiego.

Skala, A. (2016). Badanie efektywności programów edukacyjnych w zakresie przedsiębiorczości na podstawie studium przypadku Politechniki Warszawskiej – komunikat z badań. *Przedsiębiorczość-Edukacja, 12*, 364–377.

Sommer, S. C., Loch, C. H., & Dong, J. (2009). Managing complexity and unforeseeable uncertainty in startup companies: An empirical study. *Organization Science, 20*(1), 118–133.

Sońta-Drączkowska, E. (2016). Zarządzanie przedsięwzięciami innowacyjnymi – przegląd literatury. *Przegląd Organizacji, 11*, 7.

Souitaris, V., Zerbinati, S., & Al-Laham, A. (2007). Do entrepreneurship programs raise entrepreneurial intention of science and engineering students? The effect of learning, inspiration and resources. *Journal of Business Venturing, 22*(4), 566–591.

Sułkowski, Ł. (2016). *Kultura akademicka – koniec utopii?* Łódź: Wydawnictwo Społecznej Akademii Nauk w Łodzi.

Sykes, H., & Dunham, D. (1995). Critical assumption planning: A practical tool for managing business development risk. *Journal of Business Venturing, 10*(6), 413–424.

Tanev, S. (2017). Is there a lean future for global startups? *Technology Innovation Management Review, 7*(5), 6–15.
Teece, D. J. (2010). Business models, business strategy and innovation. *Long Range Planning, 43*(2), 172–194.
The Oxford handbook of management. (2017). Oxford: Oxford University Press.
Thomke, S. (1998). Managing experimentation in the design of new products. *Management Science, 44*(6), 743–762.
Thomke, S. (2003). *Experimentation matters: Unlocking the potential of new technologies for innovation.* Boston: Harvard Business Press.
Trzcieliński, S. (2011). *Przedsiębiorstwo zwinne.* Poznań: Wydawnictwo Politechniki Poznańskiej.
Urbaniec, M. (2014). Współczesne wyzwania edukacji na rzecz przedsiębiorczości w szkolnictwie wyższym. *Horyzonty Wychowania, 13*(26), 209–230.
van Weele, M. A., Steinz H. J., & van Rijnsoever, F. J. (2014). Start-ups down under: How start-up communities facilitate Australian entrepreneurship. In *Paper to be presented at the DRUID Conference*, Copenhagen.
Vanevenhoven, J. (2013). Advances and challenges in entrepreneurship education. *Journal of Small Business Management, 51*(3), 466–470.
Vesper, K. H., & Gartner, W. B. (1997). Measuring progress in entrepreneurship education. *Journal of Business Venturing, 12*(5), 403–421.
Viale, R., & Etzkowitz, H. (2005, May 18–21). *Third academic revolution: Polyvalent knowledge; the DNA of the triple helix.* 5th Triple Helix Conference theme paper, Turin.
von Graevenitz, G., Harho, D., & Weber, R. (2010). The effects of entrepreneurship education. *Journal of Economic Behavior & Organization, 76*(1), 90–112.
von Hippel, E. (2005). *Democratizing innovation.* Cambridge, MA: MIT Press.
Wach, K. (2007). Kształtowanie postaw przedsiębiorczych w programach nauczania: stan obecny i proponowane kierunki zmian. In P. Wachowiak, M. Dąbrowski, & B. Majewski (Eds.), *Kształtowanie postaw przedsiębiorczych a edukacja ekonomiczna.* Warszawa: Fundacja Promocji i Akredytacji Kierunków Ekonomicznych.
Wach, K. (2013). Edukacja na rzecz przedsiębiorczości wobec współczesnych wyzwań cywilizacyjno-gospodarczych. *Przedsiębiorczość-Edukacja, 9*, 246–257.
Wach, K. (2014a). Edytorial: Przedsiębiorczy uniwersytet. *Horyzonty Wychowania, 13*(28), 3–6.
Wach, K. (2014b). Edukacja dla przedsiębiorczości: pomiędzy przedsiębiorczą pedagogiką a edukacją ekonomiczną i biznesową. *Horyzonty Wychowania, 13*(28), 11–31.
Waddock, S., & Lozano, J. M. (2013). Developing more holistic management education: Lessons learned from two programs. *Academy of Management Learning & Education, 12*(2), 265–284.

Wang, L., Malhotra, D., & Murnighan, J. K. (2011). Economics education and greed. *Academy of Management Learning & Education, 10*(4), 643–660.
Wasserman, N. (2003). Founder-CEO succession and the paradox of entrepreneurial success. *Organization Science, 14*(2), 149–172.
Weaver, K. M., Dickson, P., & Solomon, G. (2006). Entrepreneurship and education: What is known and not known about the links between education and entrepreneurial activity. *Small Business Administration, 1*(1), 113–156.
Wodecka-Hyjek, A. (2013). Paradygmat przedsiębiorczości w perspektywie wybranych reprezentantów klasycznej szkoły organizacji i zarządzania. *Studia i Materiały. Miscellanea Oeconomicae, 2*, 105–119.
Yunus, M. (2007). *Banker to the poor*. New Delhi: Penguin Books.
Zawiła-Niedźwiecki, J. (2014). Propozycja strukturalizacji problematyki zrównoważonego zarządzania. In A. Stabryła & T. Małkus (Eds.), *Strategie zarządzania organizacjami w społeczeństwie informacyjnym*. Mfiles.pl.
Ziębicki, B. (2014). Lean Startup jako nowa koncepcja zwinnego zarządzania przedsięwzięciami biznesowymi w warunkach skrajnej niepewności. *Marketing i Rynek, 5*(CD), 736–742.
Zioło, Z. (2013). Miejsce przedsiębiorczości w edukacji. *Przedsiębiorczość-Edukacja, 8*, 10–23.

CHAPTER 4

Conclusions

Abstract The summary of the dissertation presents the most important conclusions from the analysis and points out issues for further research. The subject of startups, innovative and high-tech entrepreneurship, new management methodologies, and guidelines for education in this field, is a promising field for in-depth research, the implementation of which creates a chance for developing a new scientific school around startup issues, as dynamic as the startup ecosystem and startup entrepreneurial culture.

Keywords Further research • Scientific school • Conclusions

The reason and the motivation for writing this book was the realisation of the lack of sufficient knowledge and an exhaustive study of startups, understood as innovative enterprises representing the dynamically growing IT and information and communication technologies (ICT) industry. The lack of sufficient agreement about what a startup is (and what it is not) was considered to be particularly problematic. The issue regarding the definition of a startup is so fundamental that many discussions taking place both in and about the startup community remain unresolved precisely because of recurring disputes on the subject. The problem, seemingly theoretical, takes on a considerably practical form when, for example, the access and distribution of funds allocated to support innovative sectors

A. Skala, *Digital Startups in Transition Economies*,
https://doi.org/10.1007/978-3-030-01500-8_4

of the economy by the state or other sources of funds depends on the adopted definition. Researchers appear to be as confused as entrepreneurs and investors, including those who take on the subject of startups in their research and analysis. As a result of definitional chaos, the results of research remain incomparable, partial, and inconsistent, which discourages further attempts to scientifically explore this phenomenon. A widely known and accepted definition proposed by Steve Blank, according to whom a startup is a "temporary organization seeking a repeatable and scalable business model" is very accurate in the axiological sense, that is, it leads to the realisation of the sense and nature of the term "startup". This definition, however, is not a satisfactory methodological tool, especially for identification purposes, because it refers to subjective and fuzzy concepts. In order to conduct reliable scientific research, especially quantitative research, more quantifiable criteria are required to differentiate this population of enterprises, in other words, criteria that allow for a clear differentiation between startups and entities that are not startups.

The sum of knowledge and experience creates the basis for scientific reflection, which is to lead to solving the research problem and achieving the objective presented and discussed in the Introduction to this work. *The main result of the book is the concept of a universal definition of a startup*, named "the spiral definition". The shape illustrating the definition reflects its idea, which narrows the volume of the concept of "a startup" as organisations mature. This is due to the belief that the criteria for identifying a startup are different depending on the stage of its development, because "a startup" is not only a young, beginner company—its essential nature is described better by a high growth rate and a specific character of operations. A startup is therefore a new form of organisation that meets specific criteria at subsequent stages of its development. In the initial phase, a startup is an organisation with limited resources that identifies a market problem, recognises demand, or verifies a solution it proposes. At this stage, a startup struggles mainly with uncertainty, whose sources lie in the extremely volatile market environment. At the expansion stage, a startup is an organisation that achieves and maintains a rapid growth—its revenues and/or the number of customers grow dramatically (at double-digit rates per month). At the stage of maturity it is a hyper-scalable organisation, that is, one in which a relatively low number of employees (several dozen to several hundred people) are able to handle many times greater (thousands to millions) number of transactions (customers). Hyper-scalability of a business model can be achieved mainly thanks to the automation of significant tasks (activities), which ultimately means their algorithmisation and a replacement with, for example, a computer program. Meeting this condition explains the links between this business and the ICT industry. Some entities that begin as startups, over time, transform themselves into organisations of a different nature; sometimes other organisations become startups over time.

As a result of the definition understood in this way, the population of startups will be numerous in the beginner group and small in the mature group. Graphically this definition is well illustrated by the Fibonacci sequence spiral, where the spiralling curve symbolises the path of startup development, subsequent squares reflect the main features typical for the various stages of its development, and the areas of these squares reflect the decreasing population size (see Fig. 1.2 in Chap. 1) . On the basis of the spiral definition of a startup, an algorithm for identifying startups has been proposed (Chap. 1), and an in-depth analysis and characterisation of the studied population of Polish startups has been presented (Chap. 2).

The next result of the scientific research on the phenomenon of startups is the "Polish Startups" study, which is a pioneering research project in Poland. It is the largest, comprehensive, and nationwide quantitative and qualitative research project covering startups in the digital industry in Poland as well as in the Visegrad Group countries. The project is run in collaboration with the Startup Poland Foundation, which represents the interests of the startup community in Poland. The study was launched in 2015 and since then, a research report issued by the Foundation has been published every year. The results of this research project provide invaluable material for scientists specialising in various aspects of innovation, management, and entrepreneurship (Chap. 2).

On the basis of the concept of the spiral definition of a startup and in-depth segmentation analysis, the characteristics of startups at the four stages of development are presented, and specific features dominating at each stage are indicated. This is how it can be seen, for example, that startups collaborate with the academia/science in two "waves": when entering the market and at the mature stage; while conquering foreign markets is a permanent process in the life of startups. Attempting to obtain external funding is typical for startups at the rapid growth of sales stage. This knowledge can be very useful for planning the support structure for startups, for designing support schedules, and for designing educational programmes for startup entrepreneurship (Chap. 2).

The analysis of the results of the "Polish Startups" study between 2015 and 2018 also allows for stating that the startup market in Poland is growing and becoming more professional; and that the number of solutions for business (B2B) is growing, in particular those sold to larger companies. Founders of startups are more and more often people who have reached a certain level of life maturity and professional experience, as well as familiarity with the methodologies for managing the development of a startup; they also actively participate in the life of startup communities. As a result, the verification of the first business hypotheses and the business model progresses faster and more efficiently, while the acquisition of external funding shifts to further stages of the venture's development. The funds obtained from investors are used, first of all, to employ new specialists, the biggest challenge for digital industry as a whole. That's why the import of human resources is increasing, which in turn stimulates the low cultural diversity of founding teams in Poland and increases the international opening of Polish startups, while export is undoubtedly the most effective way to accelerate the development and success of a startup.

The conclusions from this research project are subordinated to the questions and research objectives formulated in the introduction and can be stated as follows:

- a startup is a new form of organisation that meets specific criteria at subsequent stages of its development;
- at the beginner stage, a startup struggles mainly with uncertainty, whose sources lie in the extremely volatile market environment;
- at the expansion stage, a startup maintains a non-decreasing, high growth rate;
- a startup can also be a mature organisation, as long as it meets the hyper-scalability condition;
- some entities that begin as startups, over time, transform themselves into organisations of a different nature; sometimes other organisations become startups over time;
- startup studies undertaken worldwide are usually incomparable due to the lack of consistency in defining the studied population;
- based on the research on startups carried out by the Startup Poland Foundation, it can be concluded that:

  – the startup market in Poland is maturing and becoming more professional, the number of B2B solutions is growing, in particular those sold to larger companies;

- the founders of startups are more and more often people who have reached a certain level of life maturity and professional experience;
- external financing of startups is clearly getting postponed, and the funds obtained from investors are used to, first of all, employ new specialists, an increasingly more difficult challenge for the founders.
- import of human resources is increasing, which stimulates the low cultural diversity of founding teams in Poland and increases the international opening of Polish startups;
- export is the most effective way to accelerate the development and success of a startup;

- on the basis of in-depth segmentation analysis, it can be said that the features that most strongly differentiate between groups of Polish startups include B2B production, obtaining external funding, export, hardware production, and collaboration with science and multinational corporations;
- on the basis of the spiral definition of a startup and segmentation analysis, in-depth analysis of startups at four stages of development has been carried out, and specific features dominating at each of the stages have been indicated;
- the startup culture, including the particularly important role of startup communities, is a very important element of the startup entrepreneurship ecosystem;
- this culture is different from the traditional business culture rooted in Poland, which so far has not been conducive to a rapid adoption of startups, neither in the business community nor in academia;
- the greatest progress can be observed in the process of bringing startups closer to the political and self-government spheres, which is the result of the successful operation of the Startup Poland Foundation created by the Polish startup community;
- conceptualisation of the startup management methodology is a serious challenge for management science, and the current scientific literature in this area is modest and lacks theoretical grounding;
- fundamental definition problems contribute to the low involvement and low degree of exploration of startups by management sciences;
- education for the development of startup entrepreneurship is critically important for properly functioning startup ecosystems. It requires, on the one hand, specialist knowledge and skills on the part

of the educators, and, on the other hand, high engagement of the relevant populations (pupils, students, entrepreneurs);

- the biggest challenge in education for startup entrepreneurship is presented by the so-called soft areas of education (in other words, individual education);
- in Poland, education for startups is becoming the domain of institutions outside the formal education system, especially the public education system.

As to the implications of the appearance of startups for management science and for entrepreneurship education (see Chap. 3), they can be presented as follows:

- Conceptualisation of an effective startup management methodology is a serious challenge for management science. The current scientific literature in this area is small and lacks theoretical grounding, while fundamental definition-related problems contribute to the modest levels of exploration of startups by management science. Startups, as a new form of organisation, are a challenge for traditional methods and tools of venture management and create a climate for the development of entrepreneurship which is different from one that has been rooted in Poland. Traditions originating in large manufacturing industry, family businesses, and small-scale artisanal production, as well as the intuitive management of the systemic transformation era, clash with the startup culture which is open, community-focused, and energetic, but also nomadic and labile, and uses a hermetic jargon. On the one hand, these attributes of startup culture are a source of its strength and potential, and, on the other hand, they can be a barrier for its rapid adaptation and development in Poland. The startup culture, which includes the particularly important role of local communities, is an important element of the startup entrepreneurship ecosystem, but its dissimilarity to the business culture rooted in Poland so far has not been conducive to the rapid adaptation of startups in the business community or in the academia. The greatest progress can be observed in the process of bringing startups closer to the political and self-government sphere, which is the result of the successful operation of the Startup Poland Foundation—a grassroots initiative initiated by the startup community.

- Worldwide, the new management methodology exemplified by Lean Startup has so far been a subject of a limited interest from the scientific community. The theoretical foundations of this method, which are insufficiently well grounded in science, lead to disputes and discussions about the importance and durability of this direction in management, and the methods used in Lean Startup, considered to be not serious by many, sometimes invoke disrespectful attitudes. The lack of reliable data on the importance of startups for the economy and the recurring motif of waiting for or predicting another high-tech market bubble contribute to those attitudes. It can be stated that the promising direction for further research include, on the one hand, developing a coherent and credible theoretical basis for a new startup management methodology, and, on the other hand, creating a common methodical framework for identifying this market and metrics that will describe it, especially in terms of its importance for the broadly understood economy and social development.
- Education for the development of startup entrepreneurship is critically important for properly functioning startup ecosystems. It requires, on the one hand, specialist knowledge and skills on the part of educators, and, on the other hand, high engagement of the educated population (pupils, students, and entrepreneurs). There are many indications that this education has been, so far, the weakest element in the startup entrepreneurship ecosystem in Poland. The so-called soft areas of education (in other words, individual education) present the greatest challenge. In Poland, education for startups is becoming the domain of institutions outside the education system, especially the public education system. This does not mean that there are no excellent initiatives in the field of education for entrepreneurship and for startups—on the contrary, more and more such projects appear. However, the scope and strength of these activities must be considered as very inadequate. The examples and best practices in this field, indicated in the dissertation, may provide an inspiration and guidance for educators interested developing in this direction.

Startups, startup management, and education for startup entrepreneurship are new research areas within the discipline of management sciences. Such a situation primarily creates an opportunity for methodological work, consisting in developing pioneering research methods adapted to the specifics of the studied objects and phenomena. Therefore, the following *areas for further research are worth considering*:

- mechanisms of an organisation "falling out" beyond the spiral definition of a startup (and "falling into" it), that is, the processes of transforming startups into other organisations; it is worth investigating cases of this type and observing the factors determining these mechanisms and trying to systematise them;
- improvement of the startup identification methodology;
- research on the impact of startups on the selected sectors of the economy, for example, banking, financial, medical sectors;
- startup competition strategies;
- conceptualisation of new startup management methodologies;
- conceptualisation of new education methodologies for startup entrepreneurship;
- communities as a key element of startup culture;
- the survival of startups and the most important factors determining this survival;
- developing a method for estimating the impact of startups on the economy and/or on the level of innovation in the economy.

In Poland there are favourable conditions for further development of research on startups, among which the following are worth mentioning:

- the startup community in Poland is dense, active, and known internationally; it also attracts startups from the neighbouring countries (especially from Ukraine) and from the region; it is evidenced by Google's decision to launch in Poland one of its only six spaces for startups worldwide (three are in Europe): "Campus Warsaw";
- Poland's debut in the role of the coordinator of the first joint research on startups in the Visegrad Group countries is conducive to maintaining its regional research leadership in this area in the future;
- a grassroots initiative of the startups community in the form of a foundation has proved its worth: Startup Poland is an institution that effectively implements the goal of making as many stakeholders as possible aware of the importance and potential of startups in Poland; the foundation is currently an important link in the startup ecosystem, for whom reliable scientific data is the source of arguments and acquisition of such data is in its interest.

It is highly probable that there will occur a further, dynamic development of startups and the startup ecosystem in Poland (and other post-transition countries), which is currently the main source of top-class programmers in the world. Thanks to well-thought-out but at the same time bold changes in the field of education and the shaping of business culture, it is possible to take advantage of the opportunity not only to create more startups in Poland, but above all to make them better prepared to compete effectively on the global market. To this end, reliable research should be continued and an effective education system for startup entrepreneurship should be built.

Index[1]

[1] Note: Page numbers followed by 'n' refer to notes.

A. Skala, *Digital Startups in Transition Economies*,
https://doi.org/10.1007/978-3-030-01500-8

The manufacturer's authorised representative in the EU is Springer Nature Customer Service Centre GmbH, Europaplatz 3, 69115 Heidelberg, Germany. If you have any concerns regarding our products, please contact ProductSafety@springernature.com

Printed and bound by CPI Group (UK) Ltd, Croydon, CR0 4YY
22/09/2026
02221067-0020